D0844215

Waking the Dead

*R*ecalling those ancient adventurers who moulded our real and mythological world, some 3,000 years ago, when heaven and earth conspired in its mystery, when life could be both ferociously lived and filled with the purest magic, and survival granted only to the quick-witted. These are the stories and deeds of daring men, long returned to the soil from which they sprang, yet by whose light our path shall ever be illuminated.

This book is dedicated to Paul Hutchinson of Clifton, Bristol, housemaster at Woodfield House (1946–1954), Sebright School, Wolverley, Worcestershire. In grateful thanks for all his wisdom, understanding and help in forming the mould.

Waking the Dead

Puzzles from Ancient History Decoded

Don Cox

Odysseus Publishing

First published in 2001 by Odysseus Publishing
Bramley Lodge
114a Wycombe Rd
Marlow SL7 3JD

Distributed by Gazelle Book Services Limited, Falcon House Queen
Square Lancaster, England LA1 1RN

British Library Cataloguing in Publication Data
A catalogue record for this book is available from the British Library

ISBN 0-9539437-0-4

Typeset by Amolibros, Watchet, Somerset
This book production has been managed by Amolibros
Printed and bound by T J International Ltd, Cornwall, England

Contents

Illustrations

Colour Plate Section

To understand history is to foresee the future.
To understand it not is to be condemned to relive it again;
for wisdom is knowledge and understanding.
Therefore seek and ye shall find.

And Herodotus Said

*A*nd Herodotus said, 'Believe it if you want—but I don't!'

Thus began Herodotus' story. He was born c484BC, of wealthy, influential Greek parentage, one result of which was time on his hands and opportunities for travel. Travel he did, and it was from around the Mediterranean that he gathered the stories which formed his book *The Histories*—an epic on the Greco Persian wars. This was an ambitious project, and it was probably while writing up the Persian conquest of Egypt that he ventured forth in pursuit of first hand information.

In the 500 years before Herodotus' birth, Greece had made great progress in the natural sciences. For example, the phenomenon of the atom was theoretically understood, even if mathematically atomic activity couldn't be described, and there was no instrumentation to detect it. Nevertheless, what others had done for science, Herodotus—in his similar systematic approach—did for history. Like Solon the Athenian lawgiver, he went into Egypt, and there inquired after the priests for stories suitable for his book. He did so in a spirit of good reporting, unafraid to publish an unusual tale even he himself didn't believe it. One such was a story of the sun, changing places in the sky.

In the sixth century BC, Pharaoh Necho had been advised by his priests that a journey by ship down the Red Sea, with land at all times kept in sight on the starboard or right hand side, would mean eventually a return to where you had started. To us today that seems

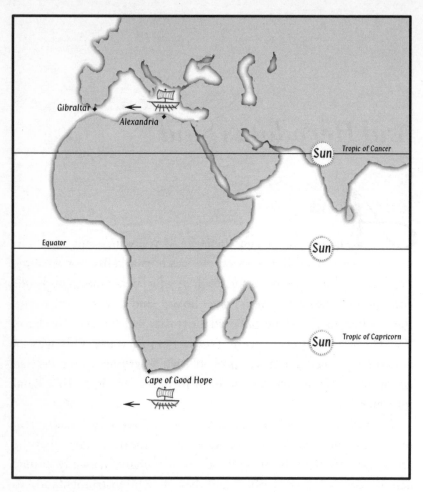

Gibraltar

Alexandria

Sun   Tropic of Cancer

Equator

Sun

Sun   Tropic of Capricorn

Cape of Good Hope

Circumnavigation of Africa circa 600 BC.

no more than common sense. Setting out thus from London and applying that method would see you sail around the south coast, up the west coast, around Scotland and back to London. For Necho this was a gamble—for he had no way of knowing that Africa was joined to Palestine, which we now call Suez (no canal in those days of course). Nor could he know that Egypt was connected to both the Red Sea in the south east and the Mediterranean in the north. Even so, Egyptians were not that happy about seamanship, and Pharaoh employed Phoenicians to carry out the voyage for him. He gave them seed and instructions to land in accordance with the seasons—i.e. to plant their corn, to harvest it, then to resume their travels.

When you think about it, a voyage of this kind was as dangerous for them as our first missions to the moon. For three years, nothing was heard of them. Then suddenly they turned up in the Mediterranean where the Nile flows into the sea. Marvellous as that might have been, what Herodotus wanted to know was what they had found or discovered during their journey. The priests told him the most notable thing was the sun changing places in the sky, which for centuries after Herodotus scholars took with a pinch of salt. Until, that was, it was discovered that the world wasn't flat, but round, that there was a notional line called the equator, and that the earth was tilted on its axis. Knowing this, we can now be sure that the Phoenician sailors kept to their bargain, and did indeed circumnavigate Africa some 2,000 years before Vasco da Gama.

At first it seems a tall order to prove that the sun, a static star in space, could change its position in the sky. Yet, if you understand how these Phoenicians saw the sun, an explanation becomes clear, and, moreover, brings with it evidence that they had passed around what is present day Cape Town, before heading back northward. At that time navigators didn't have either the compass or the magnet at their disposal, and the best tools for guidance were the stars and the sun in the sky, put there by Zeus for just that reason. If in the morning, the sun rose in the east and each evening set in the west, it was a relatively easy matter to work out the directions for north and south. Because the Mediterranean is in the northern hemisphere, the sun there never climbs to a point in the sky directly above your head. If you are travelling east, the sun will always be on your right. Conversely, it stays to your left if you are travelling west. When you travel south the sun will rise on your left, and when it sets will sink into the horizon to your right. The sun can only ever reach its zenith directly over your head when you are either on the equator or somewhere between the tropics—and then only twice a year on certain days, depending on exactly where you are.

So, as our explorers headed south down the Red Sea, there appeared to be nothing unusual about the sun. It came up from the east and arched over the boat to the west. Part way down the Red Sea is what we now call the tropic of Cancer, yet it still depends on the time of year—summer or winter—as to whether the phenomenon is observable. As the Phoenicians came to the Horn of Africa they would have been naturally forced to head east. If the season was winter, when the sun is below the equator, nothing unusual would have seemed to occur. Having passed around Cape Gardafui on the Horn they would again turn to the south. By now they might begin to feel disorientated, because although the sun would still have been rising in the east and setting in the west, it would no longer spend its days ahead of them, but rather to the rear of the boat. This must have caused heated discussion, or even fear, or panic, and certainly wonder. The whole thing would have been even more puzzling once they had reached the southernmost tip of Africa and begun to sail westward around it. The sun would now rise to their right, and not as they had always been taught to their left—and it is precisely because of this that we now know what a daring feat these ancient people undertook.

I have related this tale partly to establish the credibility of the ancients, and might add that I for one wouldn't necessarily, as Professor Jowett has done, reject the Atlantis story (as related by Solon, c590BC)—with the bald statement that the Egyptian priests were liars. It was from those priests that Herodotus derived his tale of the Phoenician sailors—a tale he certainly doubted, and which the priests probably doubted too. Nevertheless, Herodotus passed it on to us in the distant future, who are more knowledgeable, and who can pass a more fitting judgement on our ancestors. For it will be seen that there is far more truth to these ancient legends than previous scholars believed. For those with eyes to see, let them see.

The Pirate's Tale
and Odysseus Found

For those who have not yet visited Egypt, I strongly recommend you do—and don't leave it till your seventies—the desert is very hot! When you're there, listen carefully. You'll hear tiny ringing sounds, the singing of desert stones as they heat up and expand after the cold nights. Wake up on your river boat at five thirty a.m. to greet Ra as he rises full red and almost roaring into the morning sky, swiftly dispersing the river mist, much as Pharaoh once dispersed Egypt's enemies. The sun comes up quickly in Egypt, at about six a.m. It goes down promptly at six p.m., on its journey to and through the underworld.

As you travel in luxury up the Nile—perhaps taking breakfast at seven a.m. (with as many international dishes as anyone could wish for)—you find yourself cast back farther and farther in time. Even the graffiti on the walls of the tombs is 3,000 years old, for this is the ever unchanging Egypt (it is said that even time holds the Sphinx in awe!). Soon after breakfast you disembark and are off into the desert. Ra is racing towards the west, while you're on the west bank visiting the palaces and houses of the dead. To most people, that is all the west bank amounts to—a reliquary *for* the dead—but to those very few who can work upon their imaginary forces, there is something to be heard—there are whispered words on the wind.

The year was 1987 and I was up the Nile as far as Luxor (Thebes and Karnak being one and the same). I had visited the tombs in the

Valley of the Kings, which is westward over the river and into the land of eternal sleep. I had, in common with many other thousands, marvelled at Egypt's glorious past. I had shuffled down through the hot miasmic tunnel to Tutankhamen's tomb, there to gaze down on his body and face—a face that had not seen the light of glorious Ra for over 3,000 years. The perspiring bodies of all my fellow tourists, jostling to get a view—and muse upon their own demise—before resuming their laborious itinerary themselves, wasn't something to put me off, though I still fear for the moisture, and the heat from the artificial lights, combining to sustain the bacterial growth already evident on the walls of the tomb. We have allowed in an onrush of time, which leaves its mark on those who sought eternal life. (Aware as I am of tourism as the lifeblood of Egypt, I think perhaps we should all take heed that as you sow so shall you reap. Here lie the lords of upper and lower Egypt, and of time itself—so could not more be done to aid their preservation?)

As I journeyed southward up the Nile I came to Aswan. At Aswan is an enormous dam built by Russian engineers, with Russian money, to control the great river with her annual mighty flood. Herodotus had been here too—Elephantine, as it was then called—not because there were elephants, but because the rocks and boulders in the Nile *looked* like elephants. My ex wife, the lovely Rita, who had returned to me, was staying with me at the Hyperion Hotel—this is on an island in the river. We had visited the town, and with the going down of the sun it wasn't long before the lights of Aswan also went dim (in Egypt, once you have left the capital, life still revolves around sun up and sun down). We walked to the jetty and awaited the hotel ferry. It was dark except for the bright display of stars in the night sky, thousands of gleaming diamonds set in the black cloth of the goddess Nut.

Only with a gentle bump on the jetty was I awakened from my reverie. There beside us was our motorised ferry, of modern design and construction but made in the shape of the reed boats belonging to ancient Egypt. We boarded and paid our few coins, then momentously a kind of revelation consumed me—that the Nile was the mythical river Styx, and I had just paid Charon, the aged ferryman, the two coins to take me into the land of the dead. It occurred to me too that I might already have visited Hades when in the Valley of the Kings. If I remembered my Homer, hadn't Odysseus found a hole in a rock leading downwards into Hell? Here the three headed dog Cerberus kept guard, sniffing out the living from the dead.

Again lightning sparked in my consciousness, for in the tomb of Tuthmosis III I had seen a three headed snake, in reality three snakes lying side by side, all with heads raised at slightly different angles. Now—would I be right in thinking that Odysseus had seen a similar picture painted on the wall of a tomb? A picture of three Anubises? The black headed jackal god who guarded the dead in their everlasting journey with the sun?

And what was it that Homer had written and pre Homeric Greeks had said about Hades? Simply that this was a shadowy realm where the shades of the dead wandered back and forth bemoaning the fact that their lives were over. These legends all mentioned Cerberus, who acted not only as guard, but ensured that the dead made no attempt to return to the world. In Roman times there were *four* regions set aside for the afterlife. Tartarus, which we can imagine as Hell, was a place of eternal punishment. By contrast, the Elysian fields were bathed in the light of perpetual day—a realm of eternal happiness where music and good cheer were continually present. The third area was the Asphodel, so named from the pale flower that blanketed the ground. The fourth was Erebus, where Pluto's palace was to be found. It was through Erebus that the dead went to be judged before being allocated a final destination. The underworld was also a place of five rivers, the Styx being that on which the gods swore an unbreakable oath.

Homer had written both *The Iliad* and *The Odyssey*. The first of these is the epic of the Trojan War, a war which lasted ten years, which up until the nineteenth century scholars and readers alike had thought of as simply a good tale, peopled by gods and heroes of ancient Mycenaean Greece. It was an amateur, and not a professional scholar, whose name was Heinrich Schliemann, who uncovered the ruins of Troy, so that for the first time in approximately 2,000 years it re emerged, redefining its place in the pages of history. (That was the point at which Schliemann was officially promoted to the status of scholar.)

Is it worth asking, that if Troy existed, why couldn't also these heroes of old? The oral tradition has ensured that the story of the Trojan War has been passed down to us through the centuries, Homer, between about 800 and 700BC, setting it down for the first time in writing. I recommend the translated version according to T E Lawrence (better known as Lawrence of Arabia). The epic itself I have come to regard as an on the spot record of Mycenaean Greeks and Trojans at war—by which I mean I think it unlikely that this could ever have been a fiction. All this happened, and the gore and the blood were real.

Who were these Mycenaean Greeks? It is I believe better not to think of them in any classic sense, since in truth they were brutal killers. I liken them to the Vikings of the ninth century AD—but touchy about their pedigree, and keen to be identified as the sons of one god or another. Mostly they were bullies, and acted with heroism only when holding the trump cards. If they wanted to flee the field then they did so without loss of honour, provided it was understood that this was according to divine instruction. However, whether heroes or bullies, they were at least sincere in wanting to die a glorious death in battle, just so long as it was highly visible and likely to be sung for centuries to come. Thus they have made their impression, surviving as seafaring heroes, after whom we still name battleships, cruisers and destroyers. So live on, proud Agamemnon, cunning Odysseus, brave Achilles, formidable Ajax! Don't allow the shadows of Hades to dim your glorious past.

After *The Iliad* comes *The Odyssey*, a narrative describing the ten years of Odysseus's wanderings after the Trojan War. According to Odysseus, the gods in their anger made him travel all over the Mediterranean, in every conceivable way except the way home. That was Ithaca, where his beloved wife Penelope and son Telemachus awaited him. What a wonderful story this is. For centuries men have been searching for the mythical places he visited—places he was either held captive by giants or entrapped by beautiful enchantresses. In my view none of these places exists—not at least in the way they're described. To understand this we must understand Odysseus. To have called him a liar, a cheat, devious, double dealing, and above all cunning, would have been to see him weep with pleasure, for all of these he certainly was. A close reading of *The Odyssey* shows clearly that when Odysseus is supposed to be telling the truth, he lies—when he tells a lie, he in fact tells the truth.

However, before unravelling this detective story, let us put this theory to the test. We should get into perspective the Egyptian history that unfolded around Odysseus at this time. The Trojan War was from 1200 to 1190BC. Pharaoh Ramesses III came to the Egyptian throne in 1194 and was beset, almost immediately, by the invasion of the Sea People—whom he successfully repelled. This counter blow, however effective temporarily, couldn't in the long run deter the aggressors. In the fifth year of his reign (1189—one year after the Trojan War) Libya was host to a concentration of hostile tribes—or Sea People. It was the Sea People who attacked the Egyptian garrison at a place believed to be Canopus, where the Nile debouches. Their intention was to push on from there as far as Memphis. Ramesses quickly surrounded the invaders, trapped them in swampy ground and slaughtered them so effectively that the whole race of Sea People it seemed must perish. However, whatever satisfaction resulted from this victory was destined to be short lived—for this was only the first of the struggles Ramesses III had to endure. Interestingly, Canopus the place is reputed to be named after Canopus, the helmsman to Menelaus, and reputedly killed fighting there.

The invasion in fact brought with it a coalition of several wandering peoples, whose ancestors had previously been made homeless by the great eruption of Thira in 1450, some 250 years before that covered the eastern part of Crete in ash, which resulted in the collapse of the Minoans, a nation of sea traders (discovered only in AD1900 by Sir Arthur Evans, through his excavations at Knossos). This allowed the Mycenaean Greeks or the Achaeans of Homer to take to the sea. The Minoans had themselves migrated to Libya in north Africa, to mainland

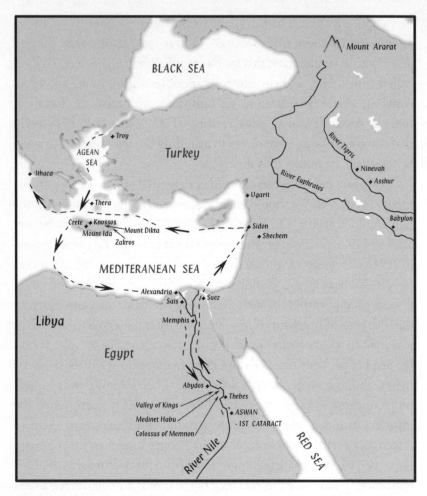

Odysseus' Route circa 1190BC _ _ _ _ _ _

Greece, to Italy to become the Etruscans and to Palestine to become the Phoenicians. I strongly suspect that Noah—or rather the tribe of Noah, since I don't think of him as an individual—was one such branch.

The Minoans had a peculiar hairstyle, as shown by their wall paintings and on the tombs of Egyptian nobles during Tuthmosis' reign. It was a coiffure that encompassed long side locks, and was shared by other people, such as the Libyans, the Hebrews, and the

Danaans of the Trojan War. These locks on the Danaans were called love tresses by the Achaean Greeks.

When Telemachus, the son of Odysseus, went out looking for his father, he met Menelaus—husband of the beautiful Helen of Troy. Menelaus told him that he'd been in Libya and Egypt for eight years, and had travelled right up the Nile to Thebes (Luxor and Karnak being one and the same). He had received, he said, many precious gifts from Alcandre and from her husband, Polybus (who lived in Thebes). We also know from Egyptian records that although Ramesses threw the Libyans out, he didn't destroy them, so that many marauding bands were left to devastate his lands. We also know that Ramesses employed some of these invaders as mercenaries, more as a policing force in southern Egypt, well away from their invading comrades in the delta.

If that was so, Menelaus *might* have come as an invader, though quickly changing sides according to potential for profit. Somehow I think these expensive gifts from Polybus and his wife were in reality payment for policing Thebes, with just a hint of a protection racket. I go further, and say that Helen was there in Egypt with her husband, and this begs the question that if *they* could go to Egypt, why couldn't also our hero Odysseus? He could, of course—though his wife Penelope was sitting at home miserably weaving away and fighting off a swarm of suitors. Problem is, what do you tell your wife when you're late home from the office? Odysseus had to go farther than that, and somehow explain away a *ten year* absence!

Fortunately his race believed in gods, and in humans as the playthings of fate, and very much in the hands of the gods, or subject to their whims. So for Odysseus the gods were to be his alibi, the cause of his being blown hither and thither, into mystical lands his wife would never identify, just as scholars today are as easily hoodwinked. There is good reason for this, since scholars have a tendency to reconstruct his journeys in an attempt to pinpoint the places that seem to conform to his own account of them. Deceive as he may, there are odd grains of truth our hero cunningly peppers his stories with. This is why I say that what we ought to be looking for is the truth in Odysseus's lies and the lies in his truth telling. So before our adventure can begin, let me try to distinguish the two.

Having got back to his own island of Ithaca, Odysseus was still his old cunning self. He donned the disguise of a Cretan pirate, began spying out the land, and checked up not only on his wife but on her many suitors too, all of whom were eager to gain control of his estate (to this end they had even planned to kill Telemachus on his return from Menelaus). It was soon clear to Odysseus that to trust in anyone was a dangerous thing, including his old swineherd Eumaeus, who anyway failed to recognise him. Odysseus made camp in his hut, with its pigs and its open fire. Eumaeus asked him who he was. Odysseus answered advisedly:

> 'I will be plain with you…Let me admit to being a Cretan son of a rich man…but labour I never could abide, nor the husbandry which breeds healthy children. My fancies were set upon galleys and wars, pikes and burnished javelins, the deadly toys that bring shivers to men of ordinary souls.'

There I think we have the true Odysseus, not in name but in the guise of a Cretan pirate. He then went on to say:

> 'Before the prime of Achaea went up to battle against Troy, I had nine times commanded men and warships on foreign expeditions…. Consequently, when farseeing Zeus finally imagined this dread course (the Trojan War)…it was for me and famous Idomeneus to lead their fleet to Ilium.'

Ilium was the Greek name for Troy. Odysseus continued:

> 'I fought in the Trojan war for ten years. Then I spent a month with my children and faithful wife and goods. Then my heart prompted me to take my faithful companies and sail against Egypt. I commissioned nine vessels. Crews I rallied quickly. For six days we feasted, and on the seventh

set out from Crete. Five days later we made the smooth flowing river which is Egypt, and into its stream I brought our fleet. I anchored it there and ordered my trusty fellows to stand by on ship guard, and I put out watchers into picket posts about. But the men gave themselves up to their baser instincts and the prompting of their passions. In a trice they were ravaging the rich Egyptian countryside, killing the men and carrying off women and children. An alarm went up in the town, and a war cry raised the people, who poured out against us at the first show of dawn. The entire valley filled with foot and horsemen and the glint of bronze. Thunder loving Zeus crumbled my men into shameful flight, leaving no single one of them the courage to stand firm and face it out. Disaster seemed to beset us on every side. Many of our company perished at the Egyptians' keen weapons, many others were led living into captivity, there to labour under duress. As for me, I had an inspiration from Zeus himself—yet would rather I had then died and met my final end in Egypt, for since that day my abode has been the house of sorrow.'

By this I deduce he was held captive in Thebes, well away from the delta and his former comrades, and as a mercenary for Pharaoh. He went on:

'My well wrought helm I hurriedly did off, and let fall the shield from my shoulders. Away went the spear from my hand, while I ran over to the king's car to embrace his knees and kiss them. He drew me to him and had mercy upon me, seating me all tearful as I was on the floor of his chariot. Then he took me to his palace, through the hate maddened throng, whose blood lust had set ever against my life. He drove them all back in his reverence to Zeus, whose wrath soon rises when strangers in protection are outraged. So there for seven years I remained, amassing great wealth, for all Egypt gave me gifts.'

This is exactly as Menelaus had done, but were they gifts or were they soldier's pay, or even bribes or extortion?

I think that Odysseus was at Ramesses' first battle with the Sea People, thought to be at Canopus in the delta, but that was in the fifth year of his reign—i.e. 1189BC. For eight years Odysseus remained in Egypt, where aside from his first landing he recorded no fighting, which from Pharaoh's viewpoint would have been counter productive. Pharaoh wanted troops he could trust, primarily Egyptians—so in stripping back his garrisons inland he set his mercenaries to guard and police the interior. I am relatively certain that both Menelaus and Odysseus were in Thebes.

As Leonard Cottrell says, the Libyans had been known before to come out of the desert to attack Thebes. Archaeologists confirm that captives from such conflicts were used, at Medinet Habu, in Thebes, to build Ramesses III's temple of victory—one of few occasions when the Egyptians used slaves. Perhaps while in Thebes Odysseus visited the slave gangs (to find out about his men), and in so doing saw the wall carvings depicting victorious Ramesses III—in the likeness that he would later use as Hercules. In his book *Warrior Pharaohs* Cottrell states: 'It seems highly probable that in the thirteenth century BC the Mycenaeans served as mercenaries in Pharaoh's armies (Ramesses II) and even earlier than that…Crete had fallen to the Mycenaeans some 300 years earlier, and now it was their turn to be thrust out. They were all on the move (to collide with Ramesses III in Egypt), the Trojans, the Canaan and the Achaiwasha'—the latter being the Achaeans mentioned by Homer. From Egyptian records we can assume that Ramesses was obsessed with this invasion and with the capture of Prince Meshsher, son of King Kaper. The king was also captured and begged Ramesses to spare his son, but they executed the prince in front of his father's eyes, while Kaper was put in chains and condemned to slavery. That so, our cunning hero knew when to change sides. I believe therefore that Odysseus was indeed a mercenary in Egypt.

There are one or two little snippets to indicate precisely what he was doing there, from his own fanciful tales—and as I have said, these were adventurers very like our own Vikings, given to rape, plunder and pillage. Bad luck at these activities meant a final reward at Valhalla, or for the Greeks Hades, as Odysseus well knew. His trade not being that of farmer, or merchant, there was only one asset he could sell— his warriors under his own warlike person. Let us now take a look at one of these mythical adventures our hero is supposed to have undertaken. It was to Hades that Odysseus was told to go, if he ever wanted to return home. Yet in the legends of ancient Greece, there were few who survived such a trip. As an Egyptian poem puts it, written some 4,000 years ago:

Make merry, but do not tire yourself with it,
Remember, it is not given to man to take his goods with him.
No one goes away and then comes back.

There was of course Persephone, daughter of the corn goddess Demeter, who came back for six months each year. It was Demeter who had taught man how to plough, to sow and to grow cereals, and it was Persephone whom Pluto kidnapped and whisked away into the depths of his kingdom. Demeter was so angry she refused to let the crops grow until the gods forced Pluto to release her daughter. In the end the gods relented, and confronted Pluto, who after a great deal of pressure did finally agree to allow Persephone back into the sunlight. This though was only for six months of each year, after which she must again return to him below. Legend had it by this that Persephone herself was the young crops springing up each year. With the autumn, and that season's general withering away, went Persephone back into Pluto's domain.

According to Homer, Circe gave directions to Odysseus, telling him that in order to get to Hades he must first cross the river Ocean— a river that supposedly encircled the world, in reality an ocean, and likely to be the Mediterranean. He was then to beach his ship on Persephone's shore, or Egypt.

What makes me think that Egypt was Persephone's shore? Well, what better country could you find to associate Persephone the corn goddess with, since Egypt was the bread basket of the ancient Mediterranean world...

From here Odysseus would find the river Styx, or river of unbreakable oaths—that by which the gods swore. According to other legends, you waited here for Charon, who would ferry you in his boat only if you had the passage money on your lips at death, and were therefore duly and properly buried (those who hadn't been buried must wander the earth in torment for a hundred years). Once over the other side you found the most secret part of the land, a hole in a rock being the entrance to Pluto's dark realm. As you entered you were confronted with Cerberus, a three headed dog, who could smell out the dead from the living. It was he who allowed you to pass, and it was he who prevented you from coming back.

The more I thought about it, the more I felt able to explain this mythology. It seemed so obvious. You cross the Mediterranean and come to Egypt's shore, and at the river Nile you await a ferryman to take you across. The Nile at its delta has at least four outlets to the Mediterranean, and is the river where in ancient times the god Amon was brought out annually on his barge and rowed upstream. It is where he swore his unbreakable oath, to replenish the land each year, through the annual flood of the Nile—which occurred between September and October. Hence the river of unbreakable oaths. Today the ferry is motorised, and once you've paid your coins the guide points out not only the most secret parts of the earth, but in the Valley of the Kings the plundered and open tombs of the pharaohs. For over 3,000 years these were Egypt's biggest secret, although by my lifetime most of them had already been robbed, so many having been opened up during the great explorations of the nineteenth century. Some had been looted by Odysseus's time, and only reopened much later than that—and one, in preparation for the living pharaoh, would have been under construction (though there was some time to pass before the cry went out through the land that the Falcon had risen to the sun, denoting the passing of Ramesses III). I visited many tombs while in Egypt—those of Ramesses II and III, and that of Tutankhamen, though I can't remember seeing a wall painting of a three headed dog or of fields.

Most of the royal tombs I inspected showed the pharaoh meeting the gods, although there were reclining Anubises—all in the singular. I saw no fields, or people sitting in their houses making merry.

When I was there in 1987, all I had to do was open a rusty corrugated iron sheet (a door) and pass through a hole in the rock. The passage was black as pitch, but sensibly I was armed with a torch and a Duracell battery (no other battery would do). There I found full size portraits of the dead in the act of meeting their gods, and deeper in the tunnel the burial chamber itself. The traps that had once been set, in order to foil any would be grave robber, had long been deactivated. Also the tunnel wasn't straight. It turned several corners, making it likely that any intruder would demolish the wrong wall. Everywhere there were paintings of people with arms raised in supplication to the Ra and Amon. With hindsight we can ask, what would these pictures have looked like if one had only a flickering oil lamp of the kind that Odysseus would have used? Would he have seen, in the play of shadows, the movement of limbs, say, or the turn of a head? In this light it isn't difficult to see how Egypt's west bank could have come to be viewed as Pluto's domain. When I thought about this further, it did present a predicament. How could Odysseus see into any of these tombs ten years after the Trojan War (1200 c1190BC)? How would they have been open? And that apart, would a stranger be allowed to roam at will through the Westminster Abbey of ancient Egypt?

Even by Odysseus's time these tombs had been plundered, not by adventurers, but by the tomb builders themselves. They, for nearly 500 years, had lived near the Valley of the Kings, and for generation after generation had worked on the tombs. In so doing they had accidentally come across the forgotten tombs of previous pharaohs. In robbing them, entry was not through the obvious routes already there, but through tunnels which they dug themselves. They kept this enterprise a secret, each night adding a little more to their mounting hordes. Records of this still exist. For example the papyrus known as BM10052 relates:

They said to him, 'Tell us the story of your going with your confederates to attack the great tombs, when you brought out this silver from there and appropriated it.' He said, 'We went to a tomb and we brought some vessels of silver from it and we divided them up between the five of us.' He was examined with the stick. He said, 'I saw nothing else, what I have said is what I saw.' He again was examined by the stick. He said, 'Stop, I will tell…'

Again, from the reign of Ramesses IX—in fact from the sixteenth year of his reign—is the preserved papyrus known as Leopold Amherst:

'We went to rob the tombs in accordance with our regular habit, and we found the pyramid tomb of King Sekhemreshedtawy, son of Re, Sobekemsaf (II), this being not at all like the pyramids and tombs of the nobles which we habitually went to rob. We took our copper tools and forced a way into the pyramid of this king through its innermost part. We found its underground chambers, and we took lighted candles in our hands and went down. Then we broke through the rubble…and found this god lying at the back of his burial place. And we found the burial place of the Queen Nubkhaas, his queen, situated beside him. We opened their sarcophagi and their coffins in which they were and found the noble mummy of the king with a sword… . We collected the gold we found on the noble mummy of this god with his amulets and jewels which were on his neck… . We collected all we found upon (the queen's mummy) likewise, and set fire to their coffins. We took their furniture we found with them.'

This was the extraordinary confession of the stonemason Amenpanufer, son of Inhernakhte. Is it possible that Inhernakhte was related to Inherkhau, who lived forty eight years earlier? One can only shudder at his likely punishment—impaled on a spike or spear.

The tomb builders were a peculiar people, having no fields or cattle, and living in the desert. They depended on the bounty of Pharaoh alone, their provisions being supplied by the priests at Karnak and Thebes. So how other than through them could Odysseus have entered a tomb and seen even one Anubis? Odysseus lived c1220 to c1160BC. We may assume he was about twenty when the Trojan War started, and sixty when he died. 1194 was the start of the reign of Ramesses III, whose tomb would be open, because being worked on, and worked on since Egyptians tended to prepare their eternal resting place as soon as they could. Odysseus might have seen that tomb, although Ramesses being a *great* pharaoh, it seems unlikely that anyone would have allowed him even a glimpse. Not only would the priests have been on guard, but the tomb builders who lived there would themselves have been on the lookout for prospective looters. Nevertheless, the idea seemed so compelling, I couldn't let it drop.

It was twelve years later that I set out on one final voyage of discovery. I was going to start from Aswan and inspect the forty odd tombs there, then try the desert at Luxor. Aswan didn't prove to be fruitful for my purposes, though if you're ever there take a Feluccia across to the other side of the Nile, and visit the tombs yourself. If you can't do that then read an excellent account in Leonard Cottrell's *The Warrior Pharaohs*, and in particular the chapter headed 'The Lords of the Southern Frontier'.

I went on to Luxor and the Valley of the Kings. I was, I admit, getting lazy, and opted for a taxi—which turned out to be far from luxurious. The thing had seen better days, and probably had a lot less life in it than a dead camel. The gears grated, and one only *assumed* the existence of brakes, through the presence of a pedal. Thus with Mandu, my Nubian guide (and novice driver) I set off into the heat. I did see more tombs in the valley, some of which were really hard going—such as that of Tuthmosis IV, and the steep one of Merenptah—but in terms of my theory this was to no immediate avail. Without my Cerberus, no one would take me seriously. Then suddenly like thunder—and whether the sun had cooked my brains, or whether the souls of the departed looked on me kindly—I had another inspirational moment. I was watching a falcon rising towards the sun, then I looked up into the hills at an ancient track leading from the tomb builders' village to their place of work, put there all those years ago. I asked myself, what if the track led not to the tomb of a pharaoh, but to the tomb of a tomb builder? Gears crashing, we drove up to the village, where there were just two tombs open to the public. Both were of foremen or overseers—one of the nineteenth dynasty, belonging to Sennudjem, the other of the twentieth, that of Inherkhau. They were only ten yards apart. For my purposes, Sennudjem was too early, the nineteenth dynasty dating from 1319 1196BC. That of Inherkhau however was of just the right historical moment, since he had worked on the tombs of both Ramesses III and IV, from 1194 to 1156. Even had he died in the year when Ramesses IV came to the throne, this would still be 1163, and therefore he had to be alive in 1182, when Odysseus decided to return home.

Heart a flutter, I began my descent into the underworld, and Sennudjem's tomb. It had been discovered in AD1884, and was in a good state of preservation. This perhaps was due to the vigilance of its builders, and the possibility that it had never been robbed. The builders would all have been related to each other, so it is probable that this was the tomb of one of their ancestors. Its treasures, if falling short of the very high value of those in the tombs of the pharaohs, they would nevertheless wish to preserve. Scenes depicted were those of fields and cattle, tantamount to paradise for those who in life never owned land or livestock, and laboured incessantly in the sterility of the desert. That said, one thing common among all Egyptian tombs, whether for a pharaoh or a worker, was the pale blue flower of the lotus plant, which was painted on the walls. Were these the asphodels that blanketed the ground, which I have referred to earlier? And were these pastures the Elysian fields? If they were, then where was my three headed dog, Cerberus? Cerberus definitely belonged to the legend of Hades, although it has to be said that Odysseus only just mentions him.

I was left with my last choice, Inherkhau. With all the usual gestures, secret confidences, etc., I was told by the tombs' unofficial tour guides that I could take photos if I paid baksheesh. We agreed a sum of ten Egyptian pounds. I went down, and like Sennudjem's this was a small tomb, well preserved (not in fact discovered until 1946). There were no fields depicted, but there were representations of Inherkhau and his family doing the things they had enjoyed in life. There was a background harpist, a party of merrymakers, and there too was my Cerberus—not a three but a four headed dog. Or rather four Anubises standing side by side as one, with their heads raised at different angles. Good light made it possible to see that there *were* four—but only just. More easily distinguishable were three heads, and more distinctive still were only two of the heads (indeed in some legends Cerberus is described as having this number). Whatever the sceptics said or thought, I for one didn't expect that a tomb such as this was to be found anywhere else, and could only conclude that what I now saw and experienced was what Odysseus long before me also saw and experienced. This I think supports my theory that I had found the entrance to Hades.

I am reminded of what Odysseus said when asked by his wife's suitors who he was. He said that he and some of his men had been held captive in Egypt, as forced labour, and had been given to one Dmetor, a son of Iasos. This is extremely interesting, since Herodotus, some 700 years later, wrote that there *was* a place in Egypt known as the entrance to the Greek underworld—it was said Pharaoh once played dice down there with Demeter. Was Dmetor Demeter, and was he not just a son Iasos but in reality of the priesthood of Isis?

If Pharaoh did play dice in Inherkhau's tomb, then Pharaoh could only have been either Ramesses III or IV, for after that, and after Inherkhau's death, the tomb was sealed, closed, and remained so for over 3,000 years. There does though seem to be a connection, and it suggests that perhaps Pharaoh and his tomb builder were something more than lord and servant. Also I can see a similarity between the artwork of Inherkhau's tomb and that of Ramesses III's victory temple at Medinet Abu. If you look carefully you will see four bowmen standing just to the front of a giant Ramesses, their bows all bent. These figures are depicted exactly as the four Anubises in Inherkhau's tomb, where they stand behind each other, as one—except that four heads are raised and four bows are pushed forward. If there were five heads and three bows, we might consider it the work of a different artist. Four seems to suggest one and the same person. In any case, what better man to decorate the temple than the one performing artwork in your tomb, your future house for eternity?

To me this can only mean that Inherkhau was on talking terms with Pharaoh, that the Anubises were his creation, and that they predated the four bowmen. For Inherkhau to persuade Pharaoh to invest in this new form of art, for all the people to see, is surely an indication that he took his lord down into his own tomb to look at the original. Therefore it is very possible that Inherkhau (Dmetor), while in high good humour playing dice down there with his master, told the tale of how he conned one of those barbarian Greeks and invaders.

I am perplexed that Odysseus doesn't mention Cerberus, except to say that when he met the ghost of Hercules, Hercules complained about the labours he had had to perform, saying, 'Why, he sent me down here to fetch their hound [Cerberus] away.' Odysseus mentions this almost as an afterthought—he was not impressed—certainly not as impressed as I on seeing my Anubis. Perhaps in all this Odysseus had recognised only a picture, while so far as I was concerned I had actually found the entrance to Hades. Yet can it really be the case that when he reported his exchange with Hercules, he was referring simply to a hole in the ground? It does to me seem questionable, and the fact that Cerberus is mentioned in the Hercules myths indicates that Cerberus had been associated with Hades before Odysseus's time. Yet Hercules preceded Odysseus by not that many years, since in *The Iliad* one of his sons is said to be present at the Trojan War. We must add to this that Hercules had been one of the members of Jason's crew on the *Argo*, as had Laertes, Odysseus's father. And if we suspect that Odysseus could act as a mercenary in Egypt, and disguise that fact so well, then so could Hercules—Egypt being a happy hunting ground for Mycenaean Greeks for a hundred years or so before Odysseus.

To me then there are powerful suggestions that either Odysseus or Hercules had been in this tomb, had seen the hound and assumed that here was the entrance to Hades. If it was Odysseus, he could tell his tale without betraying himself to Penelope, since it would take 3,000 years or more before scholars and archaeologists could piece the elements together and offer a vivid account as to the events taking place in Egypt at this time.

So who else went to Hades? Theseus tried to steal Persephone but had to be rescued by Hercules. Hercules went again, to steal Cerberus, but was forced to return the hound (we'd deduce that Hercules got to know the way there very well). Orpheus went down, as did Pollux. Aeneas saw Cerberus (this belonged to a later legend). He visited the Cumaen Sibyl who recommended he descend to Avernus, Hades' Italian equivalent. Avernus is in Italy and is well known to tourists today, but in reality is nothing more than a configuration of volcanic vents in the earth, stinking and sulphurous. Psyche visited Hades and mollified Cerberus with a cake. Giving cake and other foods to the dead was very Egyptian. A family would leave a pit or receptacle outside the tomb, so that the dead ancestor could receive offerings— much the same sort of custom as ours when we visit the graves of our friends or relations with flowers.

As for Odysseus's mythical adventures, he may have started to develop or rehearse these just when he decided to leave or escape from Egypt. That would have been eight years after Troy, or 1182BC. Of the places he visited, some surely indicate the Nile, though not necessarily in the sequence he lists in his fantasies. When he deals in specific directions, but embroiders his stories with mythical people and place names—that's when I prefer to leave these issues to those who have fallen into his trap! If you remember, when he lied to his swineherd, he was in reality telling the truth, having already judged that the swineherd would assume he was lying. He said he'd been on nine separate expeditions before going off to fight at Troy, and it is these he uses for directions, though falsifying the place names in order to deceive his beloved Penelope. Similarly, his voyages up the Nile would have been to the mythical places he could also appease her with. When Pharaoh made him a mercenary for Egypt, Odysseus as a sailor would have naturally plied the river, witnessing many of its marvels— by which it was no leap of the imagination to furnish his account of the home of Circe and the Sirens.

Circe was the goddess with a loom, and with comely, braided hair. From outside the house gates Odysseus and his men heard her singing tunefully while at work, weaving her close imperishable fabric. It was Eurlochus, one of Odysseus's men—who wasn't turned into a pig by her—who warned Odysseus of his plight. As far as I'm concerned, what this denotes is Odysseus at Sais, in the delta, and on his best behaviour. The goddess of Sais was Neith, goddess of war and of weaving. Sais could well have been a centre for the weaving trade, and even perhaps the manufacture of wigs (that comely braided hair). That Circe turned Odysseus's men into swine was a detail tacked on long after his return home. His tale of the swine, as with *The Odyssey* as a whole, didn't get into the oral tradition until he was well and truly home. This swine business was an afterthought, when he recalled his homecoming, sitting down with Eumaeus his swineherd, amongst his pigs. He might also have remembered his followers *as* unruly swine, which we shouldn't find surprising in a band of warring adventurers— and anyway a commander doesn't want soft, pampered, educated men. Rather he wants men with fire in their bellies. As for the name Eurlochus, was that in truth derived from Eumaeus, his loyal swineherd? And if Eumaeus had turned him over to Penelope's suitors, then Odysseus would have been lucky to survive.

Again with the Hades tale, did Odysseus at some point take wine in the city of Thebes and meet Inherkhau? Inherkhau, who was alive at least to 1163BC, had certainly started work on his own tomb before then. Perhaps Odysseus said he had heard that this was the land where the dead dwelt. Perhaps Inherkhau told him that the dead lived on the west bank of the Nile, the side where Ra descended to the underworld. Perhaps Inherkhau was over in Luxor (which was just seven kilometres from his village and a one to two hour walk), and told him about the sculpting or painting in the temples, which were being built in honour of Ramesses' victory. This was Inherkhau's profession, and as overseer of tomb portraits and sculptures, his knowledge would have been expert. Then again Inherkhau could have been in Thebes asking why supplies hadn't been sent to the workers. It could have been the outset of that particular period. We certainly know that in 1169 and 1165 the workers actually did go on strike, refusing to work on the royal tomb until they'd been fed. If Odysseus was there at that point, then Inherkhau instantly saw a way of getting food for nothing as well as show this foreigner the entrance to the underworld, which he sought. And anyway, here was one tomb you could enter without any problems.

So saying, Inherkhau told Odysseus to take two sheep and sacrifice them in front of the entrance to his tomb. When the blood ran out into the pit, the ghosts would appear, eager to drink of the liquid of life. Odysseus purchased his sheep and headed for the river, paying the ferryman to take them all across. Together they struck out into the desert and Inherkhau's village, about an hour's walk away. On the journey they passed the two colossal statues to Amenophis III, and perhaps it was Odysseus who was responsible for the legend that these where erected for Prince Memnon, the Black Prince of Ethiopia, who fought and died at Troy. At Inherkhau's tomb, Odysseus must also come to the village of the tomb builders. There he slaughtered the sheep and waited for the ghosts. Meanwhile Inherkhau removed the carcass and took it to his family to cook, quite possibly without Odysseus knowing. In any case this was in the nature of sacrifices— the gods got the blood and aroma, while the priests were left with the wholesome bit (one of the perks of their job).

Long as Odysseus might wait, naturally the ghosts didn't appear. Impatient, he entered the tomb, where under the flicker of his lamp he saw the 'dead' sitting in their houses and working in the fields (or Elysian fields). There too was the three headed dog, which he identified as Cerberus. (One has to remember that to a Mycenaean Greek, whose own works of art were coarse in comparison, these paintings would appear extremely lifelike.) When he returned to the surface he found himself surrounded by people begging him for food with outstretched arms, and by this time—whether Odysseus knew it or not—he'd been conned. He was though cunning enough to say that he'd met the ghosts of his mother, of Hercules, of Achilles and Ajax, and of others he'd come to see. He also claimed to have met the blind old prophet Teiresias, who told him not to molest the beautiful sacred bull that was favoured of the sun god. Now I don't myself believe in ghosts, but that aside how could Teiresias have spoken of something he couldn't have known about, being long dead and anyway buried in Greece? Again, we must remember that *The Odyssey* is telling of this after the event. Odysseus's men do slay the sacred bull, so this is perhaps his way of saying it wasn't his fault, while deep down he was worried about it.

Next, we have the ghost of Hercules appearing, which is a wonderful revelation. Odysseus describes him as he rises: 'He stood dark as night, naked bow in hand and arrow ready on the string, glaring fiercely like one about to shoot. His breast was bound with a baldric, a striking work of solid gold, marvellously wrought with images of bears, wild boars and bright eyed lions, of fights and wars, slaughter and murdering of men.'

Ghost or no ghost, I myself have seen this image. It is three times life size, and in ancient times its colours would have been fresh and bright. The chest is harnessed in a sumptuous baldric of body armour, in the Egyptian style. The bow is fully bent and the arrow is notched, ready for flight. This is all amidst the rage of battle, for under the feet of this Hercules lie those already slaughtered, and those held captive and destined for bloody murder.

That likeness of Hercules can be seen to this day, on the walls of Medinet Habu, at Thebes, as a portrait of the victorious Ramesses III. This again is just right, for if Odysseus like Menelaus was also in Thebes, then over his eight year stay he would have witnessed work and progress on this temple, erected no doubt by his own enslaved men. If the figure he saw he preferred to describe as Hercules, then that was because his audience was familiar with that person rather than with Pharaoh. I need hardly stress that Odysseus couldn't have fabricated much along these lines without actually being in Egypt, or more precisely Thebes. Therefore it shouldn't matter to us if all the time he does his best to convince his audience that Egypt never comes into it. The impression he gives, of being at sea, or marooned on an island of enchantment, is all for his wife's benefit, who would find it hard to believe in his conjugal honour over a period of twenty years. Seduction is always at the whim of a goddess, and not his doing. Though of course, he can always call on real life experience, to give a twist or embellish his tales—those acquired during his nine expeditions before Troy, and his eight years in Egypt—all re shaped, to deceive not Penelope alone, but his swineherd Eumaeus too.

Most of those encounters which took place during his adventures home become more authentic if we think not in terms of the Mediterranean, but of the Nile. In that sense Odysseus has made the geography of his myths so difficult to verify that he is able to arrive home with a more or less ready made alibi. It leaves Penelope less at odds with her husband's infidelity, than the fancies of the gods themselves. I can smile nevertheless, and would love to have been a fly on their bedroom wall, able to report their conversations when at last Odysseus lay tucked up between the sheets with his Penelope.

Inherkhau's tomb certainly is unique, but I would like to think Odysseus had also seen Sennudjem's, just ten yards from it. If Sennudjem was foreman in the nineteenth dynasty, whose period was 1319 1196, by this time he should have been dead and his tomb sealed. Is it though possible that he was old but still alive between 1191 and 1182, and that among the ghosts besetting Odysseus, one was Sennudjem, whom Odysseus could easily take as old, blind Teiresias? Odysseus could also have seen the fields and cattle pictured in the tomb as conforming to the legend of Elysium. Further still, it might also be possible that Odysseus himself originated this legend—a point future scholarship might wish to explore. If that and my present theory prove to be correct, then the tomb of Inherkhau will assume a new importance, no doubt resulting in much baksheesh for the faithful watchers over it, as tourists visit the spot where Odysseus once stood, over 3,000 years ago.

Whether Odysseus recognised the village people as begging, and not as ghosts, is debatable. It was Egyptian practice to dress as gods—

with masks to identify the god you were—during the burial of Pharaoh. Perhaps when he saw them these villagers had donned their masks, and to delude him pretended to be gods or ghosts. I am, too, reasonably sure that the tomb building village people would have been involved in Pharaoh's burial rites, as his sarcophagus would have to be dragged across the desert, from the Nile to his burial place. Either way Odysseus was outnumbered, and drawing his sword fled the field. Drawing a sword on a ghost, even Odysseus would have known, was of little practical use, so perhaps after all he knew he'd been conned. In that respect Egypt hasn't changed even now. Figuratively, many a tourist would love to draw a sword on the press of traders who persistently force themselves on you.

There was one interesting conversation which Odysseus was supposed to have had with Teiresias of Thebes (or his ghost). This was the Greek city of Thebes, not the Egyptian, which was also known as Karnak, and is now modern Luxor. Anyway, the ghost told Odysseus that he and his men must not molest the beautiful bull of the sun god. When they started for home, sure enough they came to an island (which scholars assume as an island in the sea) where this beautiful bull resided. There, with Odysseus otherwise occupied, his men ran amok and slaughtered the bull, which later they roasted and all of them ate. For the slaughter, Odysseus conveniently gave himself a pious alibi, saying he'd been at prayer.

This simple act indicates to me that he and his men were desperately hungry, which could only mean that their business as mercenaries had dropped off considerably. They might even have been fleeing captivity, which Odysseus, as king of Ithaca, might have been just a little too proud to admit to. Whatever, Odysseus certainly washed his hands of this whole affair of the bull, which lends it a sense of the real.

After eating it, they soon found themselves in serious trouble, for in my opinion this was the Apis bull sacred to the Egyptian sun god Ra. Its island was situated in the river Nile at Memphis, twelve miles south of Cairo. One day an archaeologist will find that during the time of Ramesses III the temple was desecrated. If so, it was the work of Odysseus and his men, which we can place at about 1182BC.

Reconstruction of Ramassess III on his victory temple
at Medinet Habu circa 1186 BC

I can hazard a guess too that Odysseus wasn't there in September or
October, since it's during these months that the Nile floods. The gods
were angered, and as punishment struck Odysseus's ship with a
thunderbolt—with *only* Odysseus living to tell the tale. He escaped
by riding the floating mainmast, ending up on Calypso's shore. She in
turn wished to keep him, but Athena, Odysseus's patron goddess,
compelled her to let him go. Odysseus went to sea once more, and
arrived in the fantasy land of the Phaeacians in Scheria. Yet in his

story to his swineherd he said that he ended his journey after his ship was wrecked—and with all his crew dead—riding on the mast in Syria, in the land of the Phoenicians. I think you'll agree, it's a very similar story, except the Phoenicians and Syria did exist.

I have digressed somewhat, but I have at least offered an explanation of Odysseus's visit to Hades—and Circe—of his encounter with the sacred bull—and his putting to shore in the land of the Phaeacians.

We should now take a look at Odysseus's adventures on leaving Troy. In his fantasy story for Penelope, he was quite clear that after departure he went off raiding, but was driven back. Thereafter he headed south to Cape Malea, on the southern tip of Greece. At that point he was nearly home, but the gods decreed otherwise and drove him to the land of the lotus eaters. Up to the point of Cape Malea we may suppose him to be telling the truth. However, it was Odysseus himself who decided on a trip to Crete, then to north Africa. I would suggest that he'd chosen this in order to attend the counsel of Libyans, with the intention of joining them in an invasion of Egypt. (Interestingly it was Lawrence of Arabia who over 3,000 years later did exactly the same thing. Lawrence succeeded in uniting disparate Arab tribes in an attack on their Turkish overlords.)

In his tale to Eumaeus he said that he had visited his wife and children. From this one might say that at least it played on his conscience (our hero is a therapist's dream!). In reality he didn't visit home, but went off instead to Egypt, via Crete and Libya. Was this our hero suffering his mid life crisis, where adventure was more alluring than the predictability of home life?

I am indebted to Ernle Bradford and his book *Ulysses Found*—Ulysses the Roman equivalent of Odysseus. In it he lists all of Odysseus's adventures in the sequence they appear in Homer. I hope Mr Bradford is wrong in his conclusions, for I feel he has fallen into Odysseus's trap, since although he agrees with practically all other writers on this subject—that Odysseus can tell a tall tale—he goes on to *believe* all those tales. Mr Bradford's explanation of Hades, or Hell as he calls it, is brief: 'This poem was inserted into *The Odyssey* and more or less adapted to it…and it would be pointless to look for the entrance to Hell on any chart.' Yet who could describe Hercules in the way Odysseus has, without having seen that glorious colour portrait on the wall of Medinet Habu? A description that, I might add, is completely different from that usually associated with Hercules, being of a huge muscular man, naked but for a lion skin draped over his arm, and with a huge wooden club. Never has Hercules been described in armour and only occasionally with a bow.

With regard to Egypt, Mr Bradford confirms that there was trouble brewing, and even agrees that Odysseus could have made the journey, in the time he took, at a speed of three knots. But this is Odysseus lying to Eumaeus. Moreover Mr Bradford believes it's a lie, and so doesn't continue on that subject.

Here is Mr Bradford's list of Odysseus's adventures, in sequence:

1) Land of the lotus eaters, place north Africa
2) The Cyclops
3) To the island of Aeolus, driven by winds this way and that, and return to the island of Aeolus
4) Land of the Laestrygonians
5) Reaches Circe's island home
6) To the pillars of Hercules
7) Hades
8) Back to Circe
9) To the island of the bull sacred to the sun
10) The whirlpools of Scylla and Charybdis
11) Passes the Sirens
12) Back to Scylla and Charybdis
13) Calypso's island for seven years
14) Land of the Phaeacians
15) Home to Ithaca

As I have said, Odysseus was out to feather his nest, either by raiding Egypt or by offering himself as mercenary to Pharaoh. When he left Troy he hadn't quite decided what he would do, but on reaching Cape Malea, where he must turn to starboard if he wanted to go home, he did make up his mind. He decided to go on to Egypt, but *en route* called in at Crete to steal some sheep. This was where 'The Phaeacian people had formerly occupied broad lands in Hypereia, near the Cyclops, that race of bully boys who, being brawnier than the Phaeacians, were wont to plunder them. Whereas god like Nausithonus rose up and removed his people to Scheria, beyond the reach of the world's covetousness.' This is a fantasy tale once again, but with some truth in it, for I consider Nausithonus, if he did exist, was a Minoan after that time when Crete suffered terrible natural disaster in the wake of Thira's eruption. The Minoans must have clung to a remnant of civilisation as sea traders, once they had fled. However, archaeology does inform us that within a few years the Mycenaeans were beginning to settle in Crete. And these indeed *were* bully boys, compared to the gentler Minoans.

It was these people that Odysseus met when he landed to steal their sheep, to feast his men before going on to Egypt. I strongly suspect these brawny shepherd boys took him on, as it were played him at his own game, so that, ignominiously, he was forced to leave. To save face, Odysseus described his shepherds as giants, whose slingshots were the boulders the Cyclops hurled after him and his men. Foot soldiers were no match for missiles, as David showed in slaying Goliath. In Roman times, Crete was well known for the quality of its slingers, many of whom were incorporated into the Roman army.

Odysseus then went on to Libya, which may not have been the land of the lotus eaters, but it was north Africa. In my opinion, Odysseus's nine expeditions prior to Troy *are* in Mr Bradford's list, but the names have been changed. I consider he had visited in his youth

1) Libya
2) Crete
3) Malta
4) Sicily
5) Sardinia
6) Corsica
7) Gibraltar

8) Italy
9) Corfu

Then again, in my opinion, if he was in Egypt (and let's face it—
he was either on his voyages, or he was in Egypt), then he was there
on mercenary grounds, which to men of that ilk has always been a
great incentive. Events and itinerary after Troy in my opinion read as
follows:

1) Crete
2) Libya
3) Sais in Egypt
4) The Laestrygonians
5) Hades, the land of the dead, on the west bank of the Nile at
   Thebes, which was in Egypt, Egypt also referred to as the island
   of Calypso, where he remained seven years
6) First cataract on the Nile at Aswan, or Scylla and Charybdis
7) The Sirens, temple complex at Abydos
8) Back to Sais
9) Scylla and Charybdis again, as he rode the rapids of El Kanater,
   before leaving the Nile for the Mediterranean

Somewhere between Egypt and Syria he was shipwrecked or
destroyed his ship and crew before coming ashore on the coast of
Palestine at Sidon, the city of the Phoenicians. I'm putting two and
two together here, which might make five, but in thinking of Odysseus,
I think also of Vikings, and naturally of pirates. There is an old saying
among pirates: 'Dead men tell no tales.' Is it just possible our hero did
this dastardly thing, wrecking his ship, killing his crew, to keep the
wealth that between them they'd accumulated, all for himself? It is
only a thought—for who am I to smear his character!—therefore let
it remain just a thought.

Next he landed amongst the Phaeacians—or Phoenicians—telling
his story, singing for his supper, from whence he got a lift home to
Ithaca.

I have already given my account of his fantasy voyages (see Bradford's list)—

1) The lotus eaters being the Libyans
2) The Cyclops
5) Circe's domain
7) The Hades experience
9) The sacred bull

As for 4)—Odysseus's voyage to the Laestrygonians—there is something decidedly suspect about this sailor's yarn, which I am strongly inclined to believe has been grafted in some 740 years later. If you read your *Odyssey* you will find our hero describing a land where not only the womenfolk led the clan, but where the clan were cannibals. Much more astounding even than that was the assertion that here it was that the dusk met the dawn. For this to have been so, Odysseus has to have been a long way north—yet it would seem impossible for a Mycenaean Greek to have journeyed so far (the equivalent of Columbus travelling to the moon). However, there was a man who *did* make such a journey. His name was Pytheas, and in c350BC he slipped out of the Mediterranean and headed into the northern seas. It is almost certain that he visited the river Thames— or the Tamis as it was then called. He went to Ireland, and from here reported that the women ran the clan and that at funerals the relatives ate the deceased. Going further north, he described what can only be Fingal's cave, on the Hebridean island of Staffa. Further north still, he noted the phenomenon of dusk meeting dawn, when the summer days grew longer and the nights shorter. It was he also who reported white islands that floated in the sea (he had arrived at the ends of the world). Sadly Pytheas, and Marco Polo too some 1,500 years later, would, on their return, be regarded as liars. Even so, is it possible that the Pytheas accounts were in part later incorporated as another fantasy voyage of our hero and into *The Odyssey*?

Every scholar is adamant that Odysseus went to the Pillars of Hercules, these being the twin mountain peaks that sit either side of the Straits of Gibraltar. This is doubtful, since this is still a long way to go, even if storm driven. I can offer no explanation, except to say that Odysseus might have been there on a previous voyage. If that was the case, then it was more than likely he'd have put in at Aeolus (Malta) for water and provisions.

With regard to Scylla and Charybdis, to any Greek, water swirling, rushing, spewing and gushing in great profusion, was where the monsters Scylla, who sucked you down, and Charybdis, who spewed you out, lived. If our hero was in Thebes and in Egypt for seven or eight years, could he not have gone further up the Nile to Aswan, about a three day journey? Here the river prohibits any further progress, as it comes rushing out of Africa, over a first great cataract. There are many more after Aswan, the Nile being over 4,000 miles long, and I suspect here was a good place to envisage Scylla and Charybdis, just lurking and waiting in the depths below. If Odysseus had gone when the Nile was in full flood, then I imagine the waters were awesome.

Who or what could these Sirens be? Coming down the Nile, and just below Thebes, one reaches the temple sacred to Osiris at Abydos. Osiris was the all powerful god of Egypt—the god that *was* the resurrection. If you could, you tried to get yourself buried here, in hopes that Osiris would be kinder to you in the afterlife. Consequently I consider it very likely that there was more than one body awaiting interment. After all, a mummy isn't going to deteriorate that much if kept waiting a short time—therefore why make more journeys into the desert than necessary? This explains the story of the Sirens in respect of bodies on the shore or west bank of the river. As for their beautiful singing, what could be more apt than priests and priestesses chanting out their thanks to a glorious, everlasting, ever living god? Besides, it was common practice to have professional singers and wailers sing and cry for you as you embarked on your last great adventure. They were there soliciting their god, who would one day judge their souls as they stood before him. For this reason alone I think they would have sung with a good heart.

I am thinking then that Odysseus was on his way home, sailing or

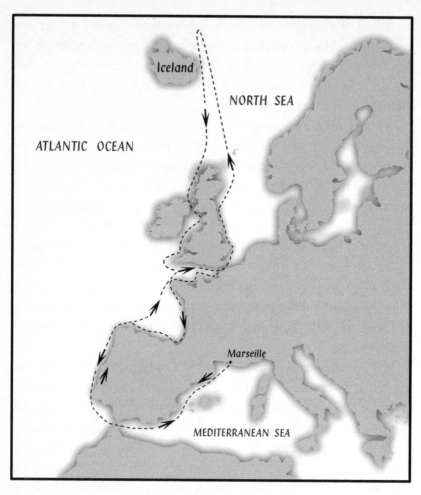

Pytheas' route circa 345 BC _ _ _ _ _ _

rowing with his crew down river. Or more than that he was escaping, having visited his men who were working under duress on Ramesses' temple. He stole a ship, but made the mistake of going up to Aswan and the swirling waters. Finding no escape, he turned down river back past Thebes and the singing at Abydos. By this time his men were so hungry they were compelled to eat the Apis bull at Memphis.

Again he met Scylla and Charybdis. This could be anywhere where the Nile narrows, though after discussing this with Sayed Abdelfatah, a student of Egyptology and trainee waiter, I am assured there had once been a small cataract in the delta, dangerous to shipping in ancient times. This was known as El Kanater, and was eventually tamed by Mohammed Ali, cAD1805, when he built a dam with locks to control it. I remember when I was told this, I decided to reward myself with a walnut ice cream, which Sayed duly fetched. I looked at it and saw that it was lemon, and told him so.

'Oh no, sir! This is a walnut ice cream,' he replied.

Being British I took him over to the ice cream trolley. Sure enough, when I lifted the lid marked 'walnut', there within was lemon. Likewise I lifted the 'lemon' lid, finding inside it my walnut. I laughed out loud, for I could see the funny side—one shouldn't always believe what one reads. However, in saying that, I rapidly wipe the smile from my face, and assure my readers that what I set out here I have researched thoroughly—it's correct to the best of my knowledge (though I feel much like a prophet in the wilderness, with his lone idea that Odysseus was really in Egypt).

Our hero had already had his adventures and was now held captive by Calypso, another beautiful goddess. 'Calypso' could be derived from the Greek word 'kalupto', meaning to cover up (one's head). In mythology she was the concealer. If, as I suspect, Odysseus invented her, it was with the intention of concealing where he had actually been. According to him, she kept him for seven years, which gives us in my opinion Calypso *as* Egypt. She lived westward, and some have put her as far as Gibraltar. Her habitat was a smooth walled cave, but we discover this was hewn, i.e. man made, suggesting a temple of some sort. Again I am indebted to Ernle Bradford, who in *Ulysses Found* states that 'The raft [which Odysseus made on Calypso's island] described by Homer is akin in construction to the barges used on the Nile.' Calypso was persuaded by Zeus to let Odysseus go, but what I think this means is that our hero was *escaping* from Egypt.

In support of this notion, I would refer you to Herodotus again, and his report that Menelaus was there in Egypt with his wife, the beautiful Helen. They too wanted to leave Egypt, but Pharaoh had quite taken a fancy to Helen (naturally enough), and wanted to marry her. Herein it would seem that Odysseus wasn't the only cunning one, for Helen hadn't let on that Menelaus was her husband, and had somehow passed him off as her servant (I suppose Menelaus *was* a slave to her beauty). However, she did speak of a husband somewhere, and insisted that she couldn't be granted a divorce from her gods while she remained on Egyptian soil (which after all was controlled by Egyptian gods). Therefore would it be possible for Pharaoh to give her a ship, whereby she could sail beyond the reach of his Egyptian divinities? If so her own gods would sanctify the divorce, and she would return immediately into Pharaoh's arms. There was of course one tiny proviso—that her servant, Menelaus, went with her. Perhaps with lips a quiver Pharaoh gave his permission, and of course, once out of sight of land Menelaus slaughtered the crew, so that he and Helen made their escape. A pretty tale, you might say! And one I think that has transformed itself through the Odysseus mythology.

Calypso told him to head for the land of the Phaeacians by keeping the north star to his left. This would be eastwards, which matches the navigational situation, since the delta is west of Sidon in Palestine. After Thira's eruption, which devastated Crete, these same Phoenicians set up a new colony in Sidon, and later one in Tunis, or Carthage. I have a feeling that Odysseus, when he called them Phaeacians, was using their correct name.

It was on his way to the coast of Palestine that Zeus's long awaited thunderbolt smashed Odysseus's ship, his men having eaten the sacred bull. This could well have been a reality—a fall out from a smaller eruption of the same volcano, Thira. In his narrative, Odysseus declares that the Phaeacians had taken him part way home and left him on a beach. Poseidon was still angry with him for killing his son Polymorphus, the Cyclops, who, Poseidon said, issued from his loins. (Interestingly the Atlantians were also the children of Poseidon, and as far as Sir Arthur Evans would be concerned, the Minoans also were—Poseidon was both the earth shaker and god of the sea.) Because the Phaeacians helped Odysseus, Poseidon sought permission from Zeus to punish somebody. Zeus suggested the Phaeacians, as follows: 'Unleash yourself, do what your heart inclines. To him Poseidon, that cloud shadowed one, do exactly what I should have done on my own accord... . My present impulse is to destroy this splendid Phaeacian ship, as it sails back from her mission across the hazy sea... . To him Zeus answered...you will smite this good ship into a rock... . Then close your hill about the city.' This is without doubt a layman's description of an eruption in full force. The volcano is the cloud shadowed one (where either Zeus or Poseidon resides), the pumice has completely covered the ship, and its weight has sunk it to the bottom. (After Krakatoa's eruption in AD1883, sailors hundreds of miles away were kept busy digging the falling ash off their decks, in an effort to keep their ships upright.) More pumice started to cover the city. The thunderbolt that wrecked Odysseus's ship was ejected material of a heavier nature, directly from the crater. I suspect that this was a memory of some past event, but is nevertheless the record of a volcano in full eruption. A volcano near Crete could only be Thira. The more I consider these adventures, the more I'm convinced they are good sailors' yarns, peppered with reports of previous voyages and previous times.

As I have said before, in my opinion Odysseus was in his mid life crisis. He had opted for adventure, and having done so met a lot of girls (or goddesses), all of whom had the magical power to detain him on an island or in bed (things haven't changed a lot if you're single). How else would he explain to an unbelieving Penelope that in an absence of ten years he hadn't dipped his vessel in a distant well?

Odysseus, at home at last, and alive, had time to revise and refine his story. After that it passed through the oral tradition, and eventually fell to Homer to write it down, thereby preserving it. Three thousand years later we can read of one of the greatest adventures of antiquity. For the next thousand years or more people would religiously bury their dead with two coins in the corpse's mouth, fee for Charon the ferryman to take them over the river Styx—which is something I did for my parents. There they shall meet Cerberus, who will let them through into an Elysian paradise.

I decided to see what the *Colliers Encyclopaedia* had to say about Odysseus's travels. According to this, Odysseus didn't visit Egypt at all—this in an article researched by a Mr V Berard. According to Berard, Odysseus landed in north Africa, then headed straight through to Italy, to the well known Roman entrance to Hades. However, this is Aeneas' story of the underworld, who although fleeing Troy at the same time as Odysseus, is doing so as a refugee rather than a victor. The story is more Roman than Greek, and is recorded to give Rome and the Romans a pedigree. Whether the tale is true or not, I cannot say, though I do see it as having evolved in order to give to this founder of the Roman people the same sort of prestige as that accorded Odysseus through his many journeys.

That said, I am very grateful for hours spent with P H Newby's book *Warrior Pharaohs*, which shows Odysseus in Libya, Phoenicia, and in Egypt, where he participated in a piratical raid. As far as my own reading goes, Mr Newby is the only author to agree with me that Odysseus visited Egypt.

Interesting things begin to occur when we ask was Odysseus a contemporary of Moses? The academic world says no (emphatically no). I can go along with that, but let us try one other adventurous proposition. The Philistines and the Danaans were the Sea People, who didn't invade Palestine until Ramesses III expelled them from Egypt. Palestine was a soft option. Yet the Danaans teamed up with the Israelites to form the tribe of Dan, which they wouldn't have done had the Israelites already been in residence in Palestine. The Exodus, as scholars will agree, was in fact a double exodus from Egypt—that of Judas coming from the delta to form the Kingdom of Judaea, and that of Moses who came from the south and waited in the desert for forty years before forming the kingdom of Israel. If we read Exodus 1: 9 10—

> And he said unto his people,
> Behold, the people of the children of Israel
> Are more and mightier than we:
>
> Come on, let us deal wisely with them:
> Lest they multiply, and it come to pass,
> That, when there falleth out any war,

They join also unto our enemies,
And fight against us,
And so get them out of the land.

Let us put this in the right context. This was written by the Israelites, as an assessment of what Pharaoh was thinking. Yet how could they know what he was thinking without being capable of thinking it themselves? And who were the enemies of Pharaoh? These were the Sea People. So why then should the Israelites want to join forces with Pharaoh's enemies? What possible reason would they have to bite the hand that had fed them? There was only one: that after years of wandering, they realised that the Sea People were in fact their kinsfolk. They were of the same stock, this being obviously apparent in that same hairstyle.

I consider that Judas's team working in the delta area joined up with the Sea People in their fight against Pharaoh. When the Sea People were vanquished, and driven out of the land, the Israelites went with them into Palestine to found their own state, while at the same time Moses' team moved out of southern Egypt. These latter had not been involved in the fighting, and to some extent were in neither one camp nor the other. Consequently Moses held his people back in the desert while the invaders violently ousted the Canaanites, before settling in themselves.

I would suggest that the Danaans teamed up with the people that left Egypt with Judas, and not Moses. Only when things had settled down did Moses move into the Promised Land. You can read that God gave good instructions as to whom they should fight, and whom they should not. In my view Odysseus was there, at the same time as Moses—not that they met or knew of one another's existence. Nevertheless the time and the place were right for them to be contemporaries.

There is one final tale to end all these tales. I poured a libation of warm, life giving Coca Cola into the sand in front of Inherkhau's tomb and called for the ghost of Odysseus to come forth. He did come, sobbing, his head covered in a purple Phaeacian cloak.

'How now, favoured son of Athena, goddess of the limpid eyes!' I invoked. 'What news can thou impart?'

He stopped and saluted me in the fashion of his time, and spoke:

'Look to the sky above and you will see in the night of Nut that the gods of Egypt are leaving.'

I looked up, and there were fewer stars that shone in the sky. Gone were the thousands of twinkling diamonds I had seen twelve years before. This was because with the opening of the great dam at Aswan, the Nile was no longer the river where the gods swore their unbreakable oaths. Its annual flood had ceased, and Egypt had entered her industrial age. Pollution covered the heavens. I smiled sadly, and for once Odysseus hadn't lied. I looked back and I was alone, waiting, like all other mortals that had come, and will continue to come, seeking an entrance to their Elysian fields. I listened out at his departing footsteps, and at last properly heard that cunning, devious son of all powerful Zeus—not sobbing, but laughing. Why was he laughing? He was laughing because the Nile will one day flood again, for the gods do not break their oath.

And yes, Odysseus, we *shall* remember you—for how could we forget? You have left us to puzzle, and that ensures your immortality, to the very end of time.

A Conspiracy of Silence,
and Talking to God

It is with apologies that I write this chapter, which I intend to keep short and fast, since my publishers tell me the ink is wet and the presses are ready to roll. Notwithstanding, I want to give you value for money.

Something has been gnawing away inside me which for a long time I couldn't quite put my finger on. Then, as so often happens, inspiration came in the watches of the night. It occurred to me that if Menelaus openly admits he was at Thebes in Egypt, with his beautiful wife Helen (a point I have already demonstrated), then Odysseus must have been there at the same time. The question is, why hasn't someone said that they'd met? Why is it that Menelaus could talk quite openly about his adventures in Egypt, but Odysseus couldn't? I pondered this, and the answer continued to evade me, until one night it arrived.

You see, there was one fundamental difference between Menelaus and Odysseus. Menelaus had his beautiful Helen with him in Egypt. For Odysseus, however, his own wife Penelope was at home holding off aggressive suitors, whose only interest was in a new wife and kingdom. Helen knew exactly where *her* husband was, and what he was doing, whereas Penelope hadn't the faintest clue what *her* man was up to.

Herodotus is convinced that Helen never was at Troy, but was in Egypt all the time. Either way, Menelaus definitely *was* at Troy. After it was sacked, whether he forgave Helen her dalliances, or met up with her in Egypt afterwards, for a second honeymoon, doesn't really matter. If it *was* a second honeymoon, it was a strange one—for when he arrived in Egypt, it appears Menelaus started to raid the land. This was odd behaviour for the lover and husband of the most beautiful woman in the world! So, to me, it seems Herodotus must have been correct: Menelaus discovered Helen wasn't at Troy, and came to Egypt either to rescue her or snatch her away.

If the battle of Canopus was in the fifth year of the reign of Ramesses III, this puts the timing at 1189BC—exactly the right moment for Menelaus and Odysseus to be part of that battle. This so-called battle was nothing more than a Viking raid, in and out, a smash and grab at everything possible, before the Egyptians turned up.

Unfortunately, and in Odysseus's own words, the Egyptians were on to them swiftly, in a flash of bronze spears. Odysseus says that the battle was going against them, when Zeus told him to rip off his helmet and surrender to Pharaoh. He then gives two accounts of what happened. One is that he laboured under duress, the other that he was allowed to roam Thebes, where he collected many gifts (obviously for performing some service). This latter is exactly what Menelaus did too. In my opinion, 'labouring under duress' was for humble soldiers taken captive, while for kings—albeit bandit kings—Pharaoh dished out nice little jobs as interior policemen. Pharaoh here would have been adopting the same policy regarding his enemies as would the Romans in Britain some fifteen hundred years later—i.e., bring in your enemies and set them to work defending the very shores they'd attacked. One may reason it so: that although Odysseus and the Greeks took advantage of the chaos caused by the Sea People, during *their* raids into Egypt, the Greeks themselves were not of the Sea People. They could therefore be trusted to fight for Pharaoh with reasonable loyalty, as long as they couldn't escape. After all, escape meant running the gauntlet for 800 miles or so, of Egyptian–held river bank, before getting to the open sea.

So why didn't Menelaus come clean and say that he'd met up with his old comrade in Egypt? There is only one answer. Double–dealing, devious, cunning Odysseus, had not only got to him first, but he'd also got to Helen. Perhaps he whispered in her tiny ear, 'If we ever get out of this alive, remember you never saw me!' Or perhaps Menelaus himself was the reason Odysseus didn't go straight home from Troy. Did Menelaus beg the king of Ithaca and his men to help him in his rescue bid?

Now I know there are some who will say Egypt is a big place to get lost in—but really it's not. We can narrow it down to Thebes, which is about four miles wide along the east side of the river bank, and about two in depth. From then on it's desert, while over the other side, on the west bank, is nothing but tombs, desert and the dead. For a couple of Greeks, comrades in arms, living in Thebes for eight years, all I can say is it would have been easier to meet than not—especially when one of them was trailing round the city with the world's most beautiful woman! Beauty I might add that through the fashion of the day encouraged females to expose their breasts.

Menelaus, who also escapes from Egypt, doesn't say a word about Odysseus, *or* that they were together. I hope you can see why this gnawed away at me, because in the end it tells me that not only were they pals, they were loyal pals. It also tells me just how cunning our Odysseus could be. Even then he'd realised he was heading for trouble once he got home. So, he thought up an alibi, which the gods would confirm, acting as witness. For how could he say to Penelope, 'Oh sorry, darling, I know I've been away for ten years—I just had to go raiding in Egypt!' One can already see the scorn in her face, and her attention turning to one of her young suitors.

We now know in hindsight that Odysseus was right. Our hero *could* play that game, the chess game of life, his moves planned, and those of his opponents anticipated—for hadn't his comrades suffered the same fate? When the great king Agamemnon arrived home, Clytaemnestra his queen pampered him in the bath, then murdered him, having already taken a lover. Diomedes also found his wife had committed adultery, and what is more had usurped his throne. Likewise Idomeneus, king of Crete, who found himself displaced. These were great kings and great warriors, but they weren't great schemers like

Odysseus (who bear in mind had designed that treacherous wooden horse). His cunning even ran to casting shame on himself, for the sake of his ploys, for when the Greeks did eventually break into Troy, and started to rape and plunder, Odysseus swore that he raped Cassandra on the altar of Athena.

That was a lovely compassionate lie, because Odysseus didn't do any such thing! What he did do, was jeopardise his own good name to save the life of this mad, virgin daughter of Priam, king of Troy. By swearing he'd deflowered her on that of all altars, he affronted his patron goddess. Not only would this make his name an abomination to the other Greeks—he had soiled a girl, to the point of making her worthless as sacrifice.

Worthless or not, she was alive. How do I know this? Because, it was exactly the thing Odysseus *would* think up, and the fact that he swore an oath, and insisted he was telling the truth, merely emphasises the fact that he was lying. Odysseus could not have performed such an act on this his most sacred of altars. He was, quite possibly, more in love with his goddess than he was with his wife. If he was going to rape anyone, then he wouldn't have done this in Athena's gaze. He could *say* it, because already he could hear the goddess laughing in merriment—just at the thought of the mortal Odysseus lying on oath. In reality that lie was a sacrifice, made to her.

By now you might be wondering if I believe in these gods, or whether they existed, and if they did indeed communicate with mortals. The answer is of course they did. However, what they didn't realise was that those voices they heard in their heads weren't gods communicating with them but their own thoughts. When a voice in your head says, "Look out there's a spear coming your way," it has to be your patron god helping you. They didn't realise the eyes had seen the spear, and informed the brain which makes you duck, all in a flash. So they couldn't comprehend that such reflex thought was their own activity. Back 3,000 years ago most of the world, especially the Mycenaean Greeks, were illiterate. Voices in your head must have seemed natural when you communicated with your god. In fact, we have an ancient custom carried forward from the very beginning of all religions. It's called praying; perhaps your god hears you but what is a certainty is that you hear yourself. Aren't we really talking to ourselves? It wasn't Zeus telling Odysseus to throw his armour off and beg forgiveness from Pharaoh, it wasn't even Odysseus thinking it, but it was his quick, no nonsense, common sense brain thinking it, for a brain is not happy about dying. Interestingly, in the medical profession you're not classified as dead until you're brain dead. Even then parts of your body go on living.

Even today, few of us realise we are two personalities in one. Just because we do the walking and the talking, doesn't mean there isn't another person in total control. That's the brain, the brain that we ever hardly think about. This good fellow will make all good decisions provided you've furnished it with sound knowledge and are prepared to let your head rule your heart. You could say this latter is your god, and the only intelligence that ever truly helps you. You think your will is free, but if you're hungry you'll find it hard to resist the command to go and find food. Try to stop breathing or blinking. In practice you can starve yourself to death, or commit suicide, but only if your brain allows you to do this by prior agreement. This is how it was with the ancients. Those of them who couldn't write, but could hear language in their thoughts, got confused, and thought they were in touch with their gods.

Scholars have wondered how it is, as the years roll forward, that gods communicate less and less with us mortals. The answer is very simple. We have invented writing, a tool to notate our thoughts. In ancient days, when a reflex action caused you to think, that thought seemed so quick and spontaneous it had to be the work of a god. Young healthy men and maidens fell asleep, only to find gods and goddesses coming down from Olympus to lie with them in sexual abandon. This couldn't be thinking, because the thinker was asleep—though in our own interpretation we would settle less for gods and more for vivid dreams.

It shouldn't be forgotten that up to the eighteenth century, falling in love was deemed a spell, one that had been cast on you. Not until the twentieth century were the full facts revealed—that falling in love was a set of complicated chemical reactions within the brain, over which we have very little control. It might occur to someone to ask why does the brain do this. I can only suggest that it's possible that the brain wishes to live forever, with of course love leading to sex and the begetting of children. Therefore for me, all this action of the brain is the nearest we'll get to commune with a god, because without reason no god can exist. (It has even been demonstrated that the brain can pass on mechanical information over succeeding generations, via DNA. There was one experiment involving seven generations of canaries, whose eggs were removed before any communication with the parent birds took place. Not one generation saw a nest, yet when nesting material was introduced to the seventh breeding pair, they built one perfectly. To do so, where did they get their information?)

What I have related is not through a god, but the result of my own reasoning and my own deductions. Odysseus, Menelaus and Helen were all in Thebes, and the pact they made was a conspiracy of silence. Homer didn't discover it, as have none of the world's scholars. Come what may, Odysseus was going to make every effort to hold on to his wife and kingdom, even if that meant lying. What better man to do this but himself?

Is This the Face of
Black Memnon,
Killed by Achilles at Troy?

aking the Dead is what this book is called, so once again I'll gently shake awake another ancient warrior for questioning. I had been staring seventy feet upwards at the shattered faces of two great statues familiar to all tourists of Egypt, the Colossi of Memnon. Except they weren't. Who they were – Pharaoh Amenophis III – wasn't difficult to discover. As to who Memnon was, the black prince of Ethiopia – that was going to mean another interesting detective story.

You might say if Memnon was Ethiopian he couldn't have been Egyptian, but the Ethiopia we know today isn't necessarily the one we need to consider. Ethiopia in ancient times was Nubia in southern Egypt. According to Herodotus, Merowe (down the Nile) was its capital, and, according to Josephus, Moses went on an expedition into Ethiopia, marrying as his reward an Ethiopian princess. Many pharaohs would have had Ethiopian or Nubian wives or concubines. So, to all intents, Ethiopia was the name for southern Egypt, and is not to be confused with present day Ethiopia (which was once Abyssinia).

As for these statues, time has not been kind to them. In 27BC the most northerly one was damaged by an earthquake, and that resulted in a curious phenomenon. Each morning as the sun rose its warm rays, on striking the statue, produced a musical sound much like the twang of harp strings. Out of that of course a legend grew, with the phenomenon explained as Memnon greeting his mother Dawn, as she rose in the heavens. In AD170 the emperor Septimius Severus repaired the statue, and thereafter the sounds were never heard again. You can see why the tale stuck for so long – for every boy should love his mother – though a rational explanation is probably that the notes were caused by the expansion of the broken statue as it warmed with the sunrise.

So, in endeavouring to find my Memnon, let's start with the legend of Aurora and Tithonus, which is mentioned in *The Iliad*. It was Tithonus who was the husband of Aurora, the goddess of the dawn, also known to the Greeks as Eos. Tithonus was the father of her son, the dark skinned Prince Memnon, who was killed at Troy by Achilles. Tithonus himself, according to legend, suffered a strange fate, for Aurora (Eos) asked Zeus to make him immortal. Zeus agreed, though she hadn't thought to ask him to make Tithonus remain young. As he grew old he became so enfeebled that he could do nothing for himself, and in the end prayed every day for death. Being immortal there was no release – he could not die. At last in pity the goddess laid him in a room, shutting the door behind her. There he babbled on endlessly, words without meaning, until only a dry husk of a man remained.

The story is interesting in that it's recalled by these colossal statues. They stand guarding the entrance to the mortuary temple of Amenophis III, a temple that has long since vanished. If you look carefully at the statues you can still see graffiti written on their feet, and put there by none other than Hadrian, emperor of the Roman world.

Somehow this legend has got distorted in the telling, and the telling has been by a Greek adventurer rather than an Egyptian. In it is a grain of truth, for at least an Egyptian is recorded as having been in Troy. Tithonus I suggest was the pharaoh Tuthmosis IV (1401–1391BC). Whether his wife was called the dawn goddess I cannot say, but all Egyptian pharaohs were born of Ra, the sun. It stands to reason that Egyptian queens could have enjoyed similar titles. Also, Tuthmosis IV was the father of Amenophis III (1391–1353BC), the owner of these statues, so there we can see a connection with this story. As for Tithonus getting older and older, until a mere husk, this to me is the comment of someone seeing but not understanding a mummified body in a tomb, one already open to foreign, inquisitive eyes. As this is a Greek legend it is reasonable to suggest that that observer was also Greek. As to when he lived, it must have been after the Trojan wars of 1200–1190BC. Interestingly it was at this time that Mycenaean Greeks started to be used as mercenaries in Egypt. It therefore stands to reason that the legend had to be just after the Trojan war, when the saga of Memnon would have been hot on the lips of singers of valiant songs. So, I suggest these Greek mercenaries, on seeing these statues, had put two and two together and come up with five. Menelaus, one of the Greek heroes of Troy, was in Thebes (as attested to in *The Odyssey*). Another candidate would be Odysseus, who says he was everywhere but Egypt, when I'm sure Egypt was precisely where he was.

How fitting if I could show there was still a remembrance of Memnon just after the war. Well, of course, there was – for it was in Book Four of *The Odyssey* that Menelaus, who had returned home, and taking supper in his palace, sitting beside the beautiful Helen, brought his audience to tears talking of the death of Antilochus, whom Memnon, the glorious son of shining Dawn, had slain. As I consider that both Menelaus and Odysseus where in Egypt, acting as mercenaries, I suspect it was these two who had come across the statues and in error assumed they were erected in honour of Black Memnon, prince of Ethiopia. I further suggest that it was these two heroes who had been inquisitive enough to peer into an open tomb and seen a shrivelled mummified body. I think they had a guide, who had the authority to travel within this restricted zone, and that would have been none other than Inherkhau, supervisor of the tomb builders. But whose tomb could this have been? Every pharaoh's tomb would have been sealed up, except for that of Ramesses III, who of course was still alive. Yet something indicated this was not just some old stiff they'd seen, for as legend had it he was regal enough to warrant a room with a door to it.

Then the thunderbolt arrived, and again I shall be cursed by all scholars, for I have no facts to base my case on, only instinct. For there was one pharaoh whose tomb and mortal remains may have been open to the sun's rays. Could it have been the tomb (WV25) of Amenophis IV, son of Amenophis III, and if so why? Let's see how you, members of the jury, feel about this scenario.

Amenophis IV, when coming to the throne, proceeded to eliminate all of Egypt's ancient gods, closing all the temples and displacing all the priests – just as our own Henry VIII did some 2,600 years later. Our Amenophis IV was none other than the heretic Pharaoh Akhenaten, whose city was totally destroyed on his death, a death that may even have been hastened by those very same priests. Do you think it possible that they could have mummified his body, but in revenge refused to seal up his tomb, leaving it open for the sun, his Aten, to shine on him? To them that was fitting revenge. After all, it is known that tomb WV25 was originally *his* tomb, and this seems to have been open. According to archaeologists, rain had washed a number of items from tomb WV23 into it, WV23 being the tomb of Ay, who died some fourteen years later. Then as the years passed and the hatred subsided Akhenaten was again moved, to tomb KV55. If this had been 120 years later then Menelaus and Odysseus could well have been present. Of course, this is pure speculation, but it must be said that Akhenaten's tomb was certainly opened after his burial, if only to erase his name from all he possessed. Perhaps this might explain the confusion over Tuthmosis IV (Tithonus), his son Amenophis III with Amenophis IV, those statues to Amenophis III later erroneously dedicated by some unknown foreigner to Memnon. Could our heroes have seen these statues? I believe they could. Menelaus admits he was in Thebes, and to be there for eight years without seeing them is hard to believe. I consider it was Odysseus and Menelaus who thought of these statues as a dedication to Memnon. I also believe they originated the myth of Aurora asking Zeus to make Tithonus immortal, when on viewing a mummy they interpreted it as immortality (which to the Egyptians it was). We might smile at the idea of immortality, but we've got to give the Egyptians ten out of ten for trying. After all they managed to get their pharaohs through to the twenty first century, in relatively good shape!

Of course it could be said that anyone could dedicate the name Memnon to these statues. Yet we can discount quite a lot of people. We can eliminate the Egyptians, for this was a Greek legend. From archaeological records the Mycenaean Greeks came as invaders to Egypt with the Sea People, c1189BC. It would appear they saw no gain in fighting Pharaoh, and so cut their losses in taking his employment as mercenaries against their erstwhile allies. When the Greeks next appeared in Egypt, c800BC, they came as merchants and traders in the Delta area. By then the warlike Mycenaean Greeks had faded into history and Greece was entering her classical period. Even so, these new Greeks didn't seem to be visiting middle Egypt in any great number until after Alexander the Great's time, of 336BC. The first Greek tourists seemed to be arriving in Thebes in about 278BC, when the earliest graffiti was found in Ramesses VI's tomb. Mistakenly they thought of this Ramesses (1151–1143BC) as Memnon, again getting mixed up with the word Mery Amun, which is on Ramesses VI's coffin (Ramesses VI is outside our time zone, 1190BC). From graffiti on the statues of Amenophis III the Greeks of 300BC where already aware, wrongly, that these statues were of Memnon. For Greeks to come looking for a legend means that the legend was well established in Greece, as were *The Iliad* and *Odyssey*.

Obviously the legend could not have started before the Trojan wars, and was certainly in existence by the time of Homer's writing of c800BC. So, we can narrow the gap to between 1190 and 800BC. There don't seem to be any Greeks in Egypt after 1180BC, when Menelaus and Odysseus had escaped – until 300BC. I consider these are the two best candidates for creating the legend, for whoever did so was inquisitive, inventive, and enjoyed sufficient authority to be listened to. That said, one could be forgiven for narrowing it down to Odysseus alone. Yet we must remember that Odysseus was never going to admit to being in Egypt, so it's only Menelaus who could tell this story. We should also remember that they were both friends of old Nestor, and it was Nestor's son, Antilochus, who was killed by Memnon.

Be that as it may, this doesn't help me find my Memnon, who had died quite late in the Trojan war – about 1192BC, after arriving to give aid to Troy, with a relief force of 10,000 men. Memnon was reputed to have performed many courageous acts (recorded in admiration by his Greek enemies), and to have killed Antilochus in single combat. Old Nestor had in return challenged Memnon to like combat, but Memnon politely turned him down, due to his venerable age. However, before the war ended, Memnon in turn bit the dust (a term used by Homer in *The Iliad*, and not something I got from a cowboy film). This was at the hand of Achilles.

So, I'm assuming that 'Memnon' was possibly the way the Greeks remembered his name, getting it confused with Mery Amun, meaning in Egyptian 'beloved of Amun', which might have been his title. His real name is still a mystery, though I hope to make a constructive suggestion. Despite his *Iliad* and *Odyssey*, Homer says little on Memnon. After further research I discovered that a certain Arctinus of Miletus, c650BC, wrote a book called the *Aethiopis Proclus*, in which is recorded the legend of Memnon's burial. Once again Aurora (Eos) begged Zeus to grant her son (Memnon) recognition for his feats of valour. Memnon's body was lying by his funeral pyre waiting to be turned to ashes, the Greek method of burial. Eos's pleas were heard by Zeus, who was moved to tears and bestowed immortality on Memnon, whereupon Eos flew off with her son.

A lovely story, but is there any truth in it? I think we can say Memnon was mummified and Aurora was no more than a priest, an army chaplain of Memnon's soldiers. It should be borne in mind that an Egyptian's worst nightmare was to die in some foreign land, a land so far away that burial with special magical rites, setting him on his journey with Ra to the west, could not be presumed. The priest would have been given strict instructions to bring Memnon home, mummified or alive. Perhaps the priest charmed the Greeks into allowing him to take his body rather than a vase full of ashes. If I'm to find my Memnon it is just possible he was buried in the Valley of the Kings. If so I have to find a tomb of about 1191BC, reposed in which is a young, dark skinned man who had died in battle. I had a lot of records to research, and a lot of elimination to carry out. It was one bit of detective work I didn't relish, and if it hadn't been for the idyllic weather, the panoramic views of the Nile, the stately cruisers churning up the waters as they headed to Aswan, together with excellent service at my hotel, I would have given up.

There are three valleys over the Nile: the Valley of the Kings (KV); West Valley (WV); and the Queens' Valley (QV). The Valley of the Kings was still in use until its last burial, of Ramesses XI, 1100–1070BC. From then on the pharaohs were buried elsewhere, back towards the Delta area. Archaeologists have found there was a reshuffling of royal mummies from one tomb to another. Amenophis III was one of many who was moved from his tomb, WV22, to a communal tomb, KV35, as was his wife Tiye. We also know that Tuthmosis IV, Amenophis III, Sethos II, Merenptah, Siptah and other mummies had been removed from their own into the more secure tomb of Amenophis II (1427–1301BC). Interestingly the priests and officials were not too particular as to whose coffin these bodies where reburied in. For example Amenophis III was buried in a coffin for Ramesses III, whose lid belonged to Sethos II, while Merenptah's base coffin went to Sethnakhte. In other words, once out of sight, accuracy and reverence seemed to be forgotten. Keeping this in mind it just might throw some light on my further research into who was Memnon.

Many pharaohs married Ethiopian princesses, so it stands to reason one of their progeny would turn out to be dark skinned. Perhaps Memnon was the child of a lesser wife. However, we do have archaeological proof that a certain Maihepri was buried in the valley in tomb KV36. He is definitely black and has Ethiopian or Nubian features, and appears to have died at the age of twenty four. We are told Memnon was a prince, but could he have been buried in the Valley of the Kings, for to be buried there was a privilege indeed? Pharaohs had many children – it was part of the job – and had they all been allowed burial sites in the valley it would soon have been full to overflowing. Ramesses II had fifty four sons and a hundred odd daughters, of whom he married four himself, though he did build one communal tomb (KV3) for all of his sons. It has been excavated, but apart from a few bones and rags and thousands of pieces of pottery, nothing remains. However, he nor his sons play any part in this tale, as they were all long dead, so the best first call is to establish who was Memnon's father. If he fought at Troy he'd be young, though not so young that he wasn't strong enough to take on these Greeks in single combat.

Pharaohs were not afraid to send their sons into battle to learn the trade. Ramesses III was a fighting pharaoh who had a son who was killed in combat, and scholars have been happy to accept a carving of him on Ramesses's victory temple at Thebes, offering thanks to the god Amun. That son is shown coloured brown, not black. Is it possible that this has been restored using brown, or was it originally brown because the pharaoh could not be shown to have a dark skinned son? Alternatively this could be the prince who became Ramesses IV and not a prince killed in battle, for when the temple was erected the battles were over.

Before settling on Ramesses III as the father of Memnon, I have to eliminate the sons of previous rulers, simply because the dynasties were changing thick and fast at this time. Sethos II, 1210–1198BC, had a weak son with a withered foot, who was later to be the pharaoh Siptah (1204–1198BC), hardly the warrior type, where nimble footwork was necessary if your job was to slaughter. He in turn had no children, and his stepmother, Queen Tawosret, took over the throne in 1198BC. If there had been another son then *he* would have reigned, rather than his mother. Here the dynasty changed, giving us Sethnakhte (1196–1194BC), the father of Ramesses III, and who could have had another son who would have been a younger brother of Ramesses III. This could easily fit the time zone, but to date there is no evidence of this. Consequently Ramesses III is as good a candidate as any for the father of Memnon. How many sons Ramesses III had we don't know. There was one on the temple wall, who could well have been the son who inherited the throne. There seems to have been another one who died in battle. However, there could have been another too, insofar as papyri, now held in Berlin, state that in the year twenty nine of Ramesses III a working gang went into the royal valley to find the tomb of a prince of His Majesty. The tomb was probably KV3, though

Drawing of the mummy of Maihepri

the name of the princely owner is unknown. Nor do we know whether
he was ever buried here, or so says N Reeves and R H Wilkinson in
their book *The Compete Valley of the Kings*. If it was KV3 then as
these authors have said we don't know the owner's name, or if he was
ever buried there. I therefore suggest that KV3 was originally for a
son of Ramesses III, but that son outlived his father to become
Ramesses IV. This being so he decided he didn't need a princely tomb
but would build for himself one fit for a pharaoh – namely KV2. Where

he had it built was just forty two metres from tomb KV3. A coincidence perhaps, but I suggest this was not the tomb Ramesses III's workmen were looking for. Their brief was the royal valley, and I think that meant the Valley of the Kings (not the Queens). Therefore I think we can discount the four sons buried in the Queens' Valley in QV42–45. However, we may ask did they die before their father? They could have died later, still as princes, but among them wouldn't have been the prince who inherited Ramesses III's estate. Ramesses III was old by his twenty ninth year and had only two years left to live. Was he reminiscing about a favourite son, a special son, a son who was possibly valorous in battle, as he had been? That we'll never know, but I can confirm old age does make one mull over and remember the past.

By now I, Constable Grumble, had done his laborious research (I did not record the tombs of the Queens' Valley), and discovered there are over eighty six holes in KV and WV. Twenty eight are of pharaohs who refused to take in lodgers. One is of Ramesses II's fifty four sons (KV5). Two are of women. One is of the seventeenth dynasty. Two are multi burials. Eight are of the eighteenth dynasty. Two are of the twenty second dynasty. Three are for animals. Three are for royal families but not princes. One is of Amenherkhepshef, suspected son of Ramesses III (KV13). One is the gold tomb of someone young robbed in Siptah's reign (KV56). One is for a prince of Ramesses III but not used (KV3). One is the virgin tomb (KV61). One is of Maihepri (KV36). Two are for mass burials of pharaohs reinterred for security reasons in the twenty first dynasty. Twenty are very small pits for which there are no details. Two are small storage pits. One was used as a dwelling. Three were used for rubbish. One was a workshop, and there are two that were false starts.

It soon became evident that I had a short list of four, all of which have a part to play.

(A) One for Amenherkhepshef, believed (by the archaeologist Altenmuller) to be the son of Ramesses III (KV13)

(B) One for a prince of Ramesses III, but not used (KV3)

(C) One virgin tomb (KV61)

(D) One for Maihepri (KV36)

Amenherkhepshef could well be the son of Ramesses III, but he was buried in a tomb that was originally built for Chancellor Bay, the power behind the throne of Pharaoh Siptah (1204–1198BC). Then on Siptah's death his stepmother, Queen Tawosret, took over the throne and Chancellor Bay seems to have out stayed his welcome, for Tawosret not only took over his job but also his tomb. However, she didn't use this tomb. Either she left it vacant or she gave it to Amenherkhepshef. But Tawosret was no relation to Ramesses III, so why should a son of his take over a sarcophagus from her, even having it altered to suit his form? More probable is it must have been given to him before she died, otherwise she would have used it herself. That said, it could be that Amenherkhepshef had died even before his father, Ramesses III, had come to the throne. To support this view, if the future Ramesses III was still a prince when his son died, then we have an explanation as to why he was such a skinflint, buying or taking over a second hand coffin for his son. It is also thought that Tawosret and Sethos II were suspected of having one child buried in tomb KV56, the so called golden tomb, but from the finger and toe stalls it would appear he was tiny rather than a youth fit for war. It may be they had another child. Perhaps it was Amenherkhepshef. It would make sense for him to be in his mother's sarcophagus and tomb, but this is pure supposition, and I have nothing to back it up.

In mitigation, if Amenherkhepshef was Ramesses III's son, then this son's early death could explain why Ramesses III was sending workmen into the valley – i.e., to find his long departed son. To be honest this could put paid to my theory. Yet it must be said, many pharaohs had many sons, and they were not always looked on with delight, more as a continuation of the dynasty. Yet he was looking for one specific son, not the four in the Valley of the Queens. Somehow I don't think he was searching for Amenherkhepshef. Yet there is just one more case, a case that has its merits, as well as its fistful of thorns. By this I mean Maihepri, who once reposed in tomb KV36, and now lies in the Cairo Museum. It was in the museum that I saw him, as near immortal as anyone could get. His hair and features were interesting in that he was a Nubian, yet he had been buried in the Valley of the Kings. It was he who had got my little grey cells working, though to be fair I was beginning to think I was flogging a dead horse. Just as I thought I had found my Memnon I found that archaeologists had placed Maihepri's death at the time of Tuthmosis IV, 1391BC. That conveniently fits in with our legend of Tithonus and Aurora, but it doesn't come up with the right date of the Trojan wars, some 200 years later in 1193BC. There had been an autopsy on the body on 22nd March 1901, which prompted Maspero to suggest he was the royal son of a black queen. In 1901 doctors still had a lot to learn, and nobody was looking for Memnon. Yet all was not lost, for there is a mystery concerning this burial. The inner coffin in which his body was brought into the tomb didn't fit into the other two coffins, the middle and the outer, which were already in the tomb, awaiting his arrival. Therefore is it reasonable to say that the two that fitted were made by the same person, while the one with the body was made by someone else? Someone who was a long way away. (Remember an Egyptian's worst nightmare.) If Maihepri had died in Egypt they would have made all the coffins together and all to fit. It so happens that my hero Memnon died at Troy some considerable distance away from his beloved Egypt, and if Memnon was Egyptian they would have done their utmost to bring him home. So, this inner coffin could have been made in Troy, where the dimensions were sent on ahead, dimensions that the tomb builders in Egypt got wrong. It was a mistake they had no time to rectify. As the body was interred, the outer coffins were discarded, and lay empty in the tomb. Maspero put forward the charming suggestion that,

'when he [Maihepri] was tired of sleeping in the one coffin, he could move over to the other.'

Charming it is, but it's not evidence. Maihepri was twenty four, a good age to go to war. He died suddenly, as one does in war, and was brought back in a hurry, to a tomb that had only just been started and wasn't completely ready. So, with his few possessions they buried him in a tomb whose occupant had already been robbed or removed. The only evidence archaeologists have in dating this tomb is its design, being somewhere between Amenophis II and Tuthmosis IV's reign, while putting bodies into other people's tombs and coffins was never a problem for the priesthood. Buried with him, among other things, were two quivers and seventy five arrows. These could have been for hunting, but they could also have been for war. However, there was no bow, which would indicate a robbery, though why wasn't *all* the booty plundered?

Maihepri's tomb was discovered by Victor Loret in 1899, and though Loret was good at finding tombs (he found sixteen) he was bad at writing things down, and left no records. Ancient Egyptians, being what they were, would have started their tombs early, so it would be gratifying to find one started but never finished, simply because the tenant wasn't expected to turn up so soon. How convenient for my theory if we could find such a tomb – and of course, I could! It's tomb KV61, the so called virgin tomb. It was hewn out but the walls were never plastered or painted. Then it was sealed up and forgotten. 'Forgotten' is a word almost like 'lost', so could this be the tomb that Ramesses's workmen were looking for? And how far away is the virgin tomb from Maihepri's? Yes, you've guessed – just fifty metres. It's almost as though there was panic as his body arrived, suggesting they quickly looked round, found KV36, removed the occupier and slipped Maihepri in. Now, there is one thing about a tomb: you put a body in, and if it's your tomb you don't lose it, neither do you lose the body. So whoever it belonged to, his body never went in.

Let's assume KV36 was an older tomb, and that if Maihepri had been put in it later then it should show evidence of having been reopened, and reopened in Ramesses III's time. Howard Carter re examined this tomb in about 1922 and discovered in the debris that had been used to back fill the entrance a wooden box inscribed

'Maihepri'. It contained an exquisite loincloth cut from one piece of leather. There were also pieces of ostraca or inscribed pieces of stone or pottery of the period of the Ramesses pharaohs. He could not date it more accurately than that, but from it I assume he is referring to the twentieth dynasty, which is within the right period and is definitely long after the date the archaeologists say Maihepri was buried. So we have four scenarios:

(1) That the box was forgotten 200 years before and was laid to rest outside the door. In that case why wasn't it reinterred when it was reopened later?

(2) If it had been robbed after the tidy up then why leave the valuable article behind? The robber, who was almost certainly one of the workers, couldn't have been disturbed because there was time to back fill the entrance.

(3) Perhaps the tomb workers had opened the tomb for a tidy up, found it had been robbed, then suddenly found they needed a tomb for Maihepri's untimely arrival. They had just enough time to make two coffins when he arrived. In went Maihepri, but one of the builders decided he'd steal the loincloth and even the bow. They then sealed up the tomb, to come back the next day to fill in the entrance. Some time in the night our builder had second thoughts about the theft, especially given the punishment should he be found out, namely a spear thrust up his rear. After all, we have what is called a policeman's dream, the evidence with the owner's name on it. So, I suggest our tomb worker and robber went back next day and laid the evidence to rest, which was soon lost under the debris.

(4) One could say it happened the other way round, that it was stolen during the tidying up of the tomb, and that Maihepri had already been there for 200 years. But I put it

to you, members of the jury, who wants a pair of underpants that are 200 years old! I suggest when this item of clothing was removed it was as good as new. That would indicate that Maihepri was interred during this later period.

Whatever archaeologists might say, Maihepri is a good candidate for my Prince Memnon, simply because he's been honoured with a burial in the valley. He was Ethiopian in origin, he died young, it seems he was warlike, but above all he was mummified a long way from home. He was of course embalmed, and I think I have put a good case to suggest that this was the Greek idea of being made immortal. Then again we have the virgin tomb just fifty metres away, which was never used, together with a father sending in his workmen into the royal valley to search for the lost tomb of his son. In Maihepri's tomb, he has the honour of royal fan bearer, which at first hand doesn't seem to be a great achievement. Yet if we look at Ramesses's victory temple at Medinet Habu, there we see Ramesses III with bow stretched and arrow in the notch, in the forefront of battle, slaughtering his enemies. There standing directly behind him is the royal fan bearer, with the hairstyle of a royal prince. To me it looks as though he is not just the fanner of Pharaoh's royal perspiring brow, but also standard bearer in the battle itself, showing his soldiers that here stands Pharaoh himself. One thing about standard bearers is they are always picked for their courage and steadfastness in battle. I'm not saying this was Memnon, for Memnon was already dead at the time of the Medinet Habu construction, but it would indicate that Maihepri had guts and perhaps the know how to command an army at Troy.

A question to ask is what was Memnon or Maihepri, an Egyptian prince, doing at Troy? I suggest that before the Trojan wars, some pharaoh's daughter had married for political reasons into the Trojan royal families. The Greek mention a certain Tithonus, who was the last son of King Laomedon of Troy. It's interesting in that the name Tithonus is turning up once more, but as a son of a king of Troy. This must have been an earlier king, for Homer is quite clear that Priam was king of Troy during the Trojan wars. It would indicate that a king of Troy in the past had named his son, not Tithonus, but Tuthmosis, implying some affiliation with Egypt. Memnon, a prince of Egypt, turning up at Troy with an army of 10,000 men, offering military assistance, is in reality Ramesses III abiding by some treaty he had with Troy. A treaty requiring him to send military assistance to subdue these warlike raiders of the Aegean. Whatever help he gave it didn't blunt the aggressors, for as we can see, after they had laid waste Troy they came buzzing down to Egypt as part of the confederation of the Sea People.

I do not say that my answers are the right answers, but they are at least answers where no answers have been before. I hope the information that I furnish here might stimulate someone in the distant future with better technology than is available to me to go forwards and put more flesh on the bones of this ancient hero, for a simple carbon dating test would solve the riddle once and for all. Memnon is indeed a misty figure in history, but I consider he deserves to be found, and should be more than just dust. If Maihepri is our Memnon, our Mery Amun, what thought can we muster as we gaze at this face, with its close shut eyes, whose last glimpse of life was the terrible visage of Achilles?

There is one final message that will bring joy and glad tidings to some future Egyptologists, and it's this. I, Constable Grumble, have discovered that the tomb, goods and body of Ramesses VIII are still awaiting discovery.

Found: The Fabled Mountains of the Moon

Since writing the chapter 'And Herodotus Said', I have had the opportunity of visiting Kenya, on a completely unrelated matter, having been invited to go on safari in the Tsavo National Park. It was fascinating to stand by the railway bridge that crossed the Tsavo river, knowing this was the place where almost a hundred years before to the week, fear had nightly stalked the encampment of the Indian labourers, employed to build the famous Lunatic Express. For here was the favourite eating place of the man eating lions of Tsavo, who managed to consume twenty eight Indians, and possibly a further seventy Africans, before being killed (after ten months' hunting). These two lions, brothers perhaps—and now stuffed and on display in the Chicago museum—managed to stay three or four steps ahead of Lt Col Patterson, and the other hunters out to kill them.

It was while bouncing up and down over the rutted tracks that my guide pointed westwards and told me there was Mt Kilimanjaro. I looked far out to the horizon, and to the mountains surrounding the park, but could see nothing particularly astounding. Only when I was told to look high into the clouds did I see what at first looked like an irregular cloud, or a weakly, wishy washy moon. And only by zooming into this apparition with my camcorder was I able to see it as the snow topped cone of Kilimanjaro, thought to be an extinct volcano, but now showing distinct signs of life.

The mountain was way over the horizon, and the area below the snow line was so hazy as to render it almost indistinguishable from the sky. This gave to the snow top an almost bizarre appearance of having been suspended in space, rather as the upper half of a crescent moon. Instantly the Egyptian legend sprang to mind, that of the Nile having started its journey from the mountains of the moon. On my return I immediately consulted my maps of Africa. If one follows the Nile—the longest river in the world at over 4,000 miles—from the Mediterranean down into Egypt, one eventually comes to Khartoum. Here the Nile splits into two—the slower but longer White Nile, and the faster Blue Nile. The Blue Nile rises in the mountains of Ethiopia and spills out of Lake Tana.

What peculiarity has the moon got that would inspire such a legend? Could it be that the moon is brilliant white? Could it relate to the mountains that were white, whose tips were covered in snow, and all made doubly brilliant under an equatorial sun?

Something told me these legendary mountains weren't the Ethiopian range. Apart from Ras Dashan, none is much above 13,000 feet, which, at a latitude of ten degrees north of the equator, would put them well below the snow line. So where did this legend come from? My research led me to Claudius Ptolemaeus Ptolemy, mathematician and geographer, active in Alexandria in cAD150. From his name one can construe that Ptolemy was a Roman citizen of Egyptian Greek origin, Rome having annexed Egypt to its own empire at the defeat of Mark Antony and Cleopatra. Ptolemy had compiled a map of the then known world, which even showed towns and cities that still exist in Britain today. It has been suggested that Ptolemy got his information from records left by a Greek merchant, whose name was Diogenes. Diogenes, in the middle of the first century, was returning from a business venture in India, when he decided to go to the east coast of Africa. It seems he journeyed inland for twenty five days, and there discovered a mountain range, which he called the Mountains of the Moon. From there he came upon two lakes, and it was the rivers entering these lakes that Diogenes said were the source of the Nile. Whether he followed these rivers into the lakes, and the river flowing out, I cannot say—it was though a wild statement to make, being some 3,000 miles from Egypt's southern boundaries. The ancient maps I have studied indicate that he had returned to Egypt by following the Nile all the way to the sea, and only in this way could he be certain about his statement.

Herodotus had gone up the Nile as far as Aswan in about 450BC, but got no farther. The emperor Nero sent an expedition up the Nile, which couldn't overcome what proved an impenetrable swamp deep in the interior (which is a good description of the Sudd area). This then left me a puzzle I just had to unravel.

From Khartoum the White Nile would eventually lead to what is present day Lake Albert, from where there were waterways east towards Lake Victoria. From Lake Albert to Lake Victoria the river is called the Victoria Nile, host to the Owen Falls. Here the river thunders and roars from Lake Victoria and fertilises the great desert of Egypt.

If one now went further east, around the shores of Lake Victoria, then headed up one of the rivers flowing into the lake at Loliondo, which is a town, then this is only about a hundred miles from the snow capped mountains of Kilimanjaro. Either way, getting that far, it is possible to see the top of Kilimanjaro, way in the distance and well over the horizon, in aspect very much as if the moon were sitting on the earth. Kikuyu natives of that region were aware of it, as covered in white flour and guarded by evil spirits—spirits who killed anyone attempting to ascend it, stiffening their feet and hands—which is a fair description of cold and frostbite.

Slavers of the eighteenth century, coming from the interior to Mombasa, brought with them rumours of mountains covered in silver—for how could these people of Africa or Egypt comprehend the meaning of snow or ice without having seen it before? Imagine the brightness of a half moon on a cloudless night. Now imagine a view with the sun setting over the western horizon, yet there glistening to the east, in the last rays of the sun, is the lofty, 19,000 ft snow capped peak. Would it not look like the moon?

Rebmann, the first European to see Mt Kilimanjaro (c1846), took great pains to inform the Royal Geographical Society in London that he had done so, with its snow capped peaks. He found himself treated as a reincarnation of Baron Munchausen. To make matters worse, and only lending further weight to his cosy armchair critics, these peaks were situated right on the equator!

In 1862 Baron Carl Klaus climbed to 14,000 ft, but failed to reach the snow line. This was finally achieved by Charles New in 1871. Apparently, when he managed to hack off some chunks of ice, hard as the rock itself, and took these down to his native porters below, they wanted to sell them as medicine. When New explained that the ice would eventually melt they all smiled and said they had never heard of rock doing that. No wonder this ancient Greek merchant, when he looked up in the sky, and saw these white tipped mountains, interpreted them as the mountains of the moon (though in truth a Greek should have known what snow was).

I needed more information on what Claudius Ptolemy had said, and for this I had to inspect his maps. By a stroke of luck I found a print of a German map of the world, produced in Ulm and dated 1486. This was in Simon Berthon and Andrew Robinson's very fine and detailed book *The Shape of the World*. It was Eratosthenes (275 194BC), living in Alexandria, who came up with a simple but brilliant method of calculating the size of our planet. Although history has granted him the privilege of being the first to do so, and by implication concluding the earth wasn't flat but a sphere, I think we would be wrong to say that the idea was at all original. I would suggest that while a student in the port of Alexandria, he had discussed with local sailors the fact that ships seemed to disappear mysteriously once they had left land. Eratosthenes, with only the approximate distance given him by travellers journeying from Aswan to Alexandria, managed to calculate the circumference of the world as 24,500 miles. We know today that he was only 400 miles short in his calculations. Yet by Ptolemy's time, that knowledge was lost, since Ptolemy made an error in *his* calculation, coming to the conclusion that the world was only two thirds that size. It was this error which prompted Columbus to make his voyage to China, which he assumed was nearer than it was. Fortunately or unfortunately, America popping up in the Atlantic saved

Columbus's neck—though already, by 1486, people were beginning to realise the world was bigger. In 1492—when Columbus sailed the ocean blue—these thoughts were becoming a reality.

The German printers of 1486 had clearly shown on their map, which was based on Ptolemy's, the Mediterranean, Europe and north Africa, and in a way that we would recognise today. The Nile is plotted, going south into the huge continent of Africa, which according to Ptolemy was connected to an unknown land mass called Antarctica. It would be another thirteen years after this print that Vasco da Gama would return from his epic voyage to India, revealing to the world that Africa wasn't connected to a larger southern continent, and could be circumnavigated *en route* to the spice lands of the East. According to Ptolemy's map, the Nile comes up from the south of Africa. If we reverse our view of this, and head up the Nile towards the equator for its source, the Nile will be seen to follow almost the exact route shown in a modern atlas. The first tributary comes into the Nile at Atbara, and is called the river Atbara. Ptolemy's map shows this as the Astaboras. Continuing south the Nile splits into its two branches— the Blue Nile going south east to the mountains of Ethiopia, and the White Nile going south. The Blue Nile Ptolemy shows heading off towards Lake Coloe, which again accords with our modern maps, although we call this Lake Tana.

The other branch, the White Nile, continues south for a considerable distance, and according to Ptolemy's map branches again. I think this error can be excused, for with my modern map I put the position in present day Malakal, at the entrance to the Sudd, a vast tract of swampland, where even today the only effective transport is by water. Small farming communities on the slightly raised lands do well, as do cattle on the lush pastures. Here the White Nile is sluggish, compared to the frisky Blue, and in feeding the Sudd almost comes to a standstill. We now know there are about five rivers entering this area, so I think the records Diogenes passed on to Ptolemy have become confused. The error is further compounded in showing that both rivers issue from individual lakes, one large and one a bit smaller, though not as small as Lake Tana. Again this is a fair appraisal of the

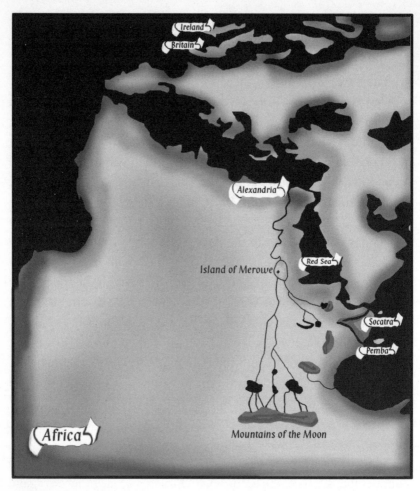

Ptolemy's map of the world circa 120 AD as reproduced in 1469 AD, showing the River Nile.

topography as shown on our own maps, except that instead of two rivers there is one. This issues from Lake Victoria, then surmounts the Owen Falls, before flowing into a small lake called Kyogo, then into Lake Albert. Thereafter it loses itself in the Sudd. If the larger of these lakes is Lake Victoria, Diogenes shows three rivers entering it from the south. In actual fact there are considerably more, but I consider Diogenes was exploring by boat, and to cut his journey time was sailing some distance from the shore, and in doing so missed out on rivers entering the lake. My reason for thinking that he used a boat is that not only did he know he was dealing with lakes, but was able to size them. However, Ptolemy has shown these rivers entering the lake from a mountain range to the south, which he named the Mountains of the Moon. The only problem with this is that there are no real mountains to the south of these lakes, though there are to the west and east. So, what are the Mountains of the Moon?

Before embarking on this exercise, let me eliminate the Ethiopian mountain range. Somehow I don't think our Greek merchant Diogenes would have headed for home down the White Nile, then—at what is present day Khartoum—explore the source of the Blue Nile. Few businessmen would have taken the time to journey home as Diogenes did, *and* give themselves licence for one further goose chase. Therefore if Diogenes didn't see these Ethiopian mountains, he couldn't have named them. In my humble opinion we can forget the Ethiopian mountains.

I was discussing my theory with a friend of mine, who at the time was surveying his white capped, frothy pint of beer, and hoping I would buy him another. He informed me that the Mountains of the Moon were the perpetual snow on the crests of the Ruwenzori range. Mt Ruwenzori is almost 17,000 ft high, in a range situated to the west of Lake Victoria. On asking why he thought this, his answer was that the River Kagera, which flows into Lake Victoria from the west, is the highest river of them all, and as such is the source of the Nile. I objected, saying that Diogenes never went far enough west to have seen them. Even if he did, why should it occur to him that this was a deciding factor as to where the Nile rose?

Interestingly, Victorian explorers such as Grant, Speke, Burton and Stanley had learnt a little trick to determine altitude. This was by boiling water. Boys and girls today know that water at sea level boils at a hundred degrees centigrade. The higher you are, the lower the boiling point. This means that boiling still does occur, although the water doesn't become so hot. For example water boiled on Mt Everest is just lukewarm. So, here was a ready made method by which explorers could estimate their altitude. As Speke discovered, Lake Victoria was high enough to flow out and become the Nile. As for the snow capped peaks of the Ruwenzori range, the least we could say is that someone was using their appearance to suggest the name—i.e., the Mountains of the Moon. Nevertheless, it did leave open the question of who it was that had coined it.

Did I buy my friend a pint? Of course I did! He was the only one here listening to me, and for that matter the only person I had come across who had heard of the Mountains of the Moon (God bless Brian Cheryl for he has already crossed over the Styx!).

Before I go on I would like to digress, with a tale of my own. I was invited out by my daughter Claudia and her husband Matthew, and we all went, together with my two grandsons, to the seaside. While there, on the windswept beach of the Witterings, my son in law drew in the sand the letter G, then asked his son what it was. Immediately we heard G is for Granddad. Matthew then drew an M, which he hoped would produce M for Matthew. He got a W instead. I laughed, and immediately saw that since Oliver, my grandson, was standing opposite to Matthew, the M would have looked like a W. What better way of explaining what I am about to relate—when it's the way you see things that counts!

So, here we have it, that the Mountains of the Moon are established on our present day map of Africa as of the Ruwenzori range. Who had made this statement? None other than the great Stanley—the very same who had gone out looking for Livingstone. Stanley had sought his fortune in America, as a reporter, and finally had his stroke of luck on finding and rescuing the explorer and missionary David Livingstone, lost in the heart of darkest Africa (those immortalised words, 'Dr Livingstone, I presume.'). It's quite daunting to have to say that Stanley was wrong, but wrong I am sure he was. He had obviously heard of the Mountains of the Moon, and like me had made the visual connection. Unlike me, he wasn't aware of how Ptolemy had learned about these mountains. What Stanley was doing was looking at an M and coming up with a W—that is, coming at it from the wrong direction.

There was one other occasion when he had set out to rescue a man

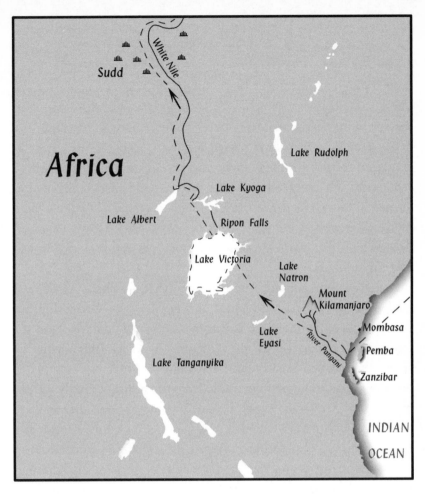

Diogenes' route circa 70 AD – – – – – –

isolated in central Africa—a person by the name of Emin Pasha. This time Stanley was heading for central Africa not from the east coast, and the Indian Ocean side, but from the west, or the Atlantic seaboard. He was making for Lake Victoria and opening up uncharted territories as he went. Consequently, when he came to the Ruwenzori mountains, he saw the snow capped ridge, then Lake Victoria, then putting two and two together assumed these were the Mountains of the Moon. Now research I love, and research I have carried out. Here was Diogenes, who had travelled inland from the Indian Ocean for twenty five days, obviously going west. Here we have Stanley, who travelled for months going east. Both see the Mountains of the Moon before seeing the lakes. The lakes are the common factor, being the same lakes, though approached from two opposing directions. Now to be fair it was Diogenes who named these mountains, therefore they lie to the east of the lakes, and not as Stanley has it to the west. Nevertheless, it was Stanley's claim that passed into writ, since on his return to England he was granted an honorary degree from Cambridge University, was knighted by Queen Victoria (and incidentally bought a house at Furze Hill near Pirbright, naming a pond and hillock there Stanley's Pool and the Mountains of the Moon). However, much though his glory was, I am sure he was wrong, and in so saying will offer my reasons.

Diogenes was coming from India to Africa in about AD50, and landed on the east coast. I doubt if he was sailing in a Greek ship, but rather in an Arab dhow, for it was the Arabs who monopolised sea trade before the arrival of the white man in Africa (this was in the sixteenth century). Slavery had been going on for centuries, and it is possible it was still going on in Diogenes' time. Interestingly we can narrow it down to the time of year, for one natural phenomenon associated with Africa—then as now—is its two winds. Almost as a regular dynamo, from October to April, the winds blow from the north east—almost a direct run from India and the Persian Gulf to Zanzibar. This is the Kazkazi, which from May to September reverses itself to blow from the south west, allowing sailing ships to return from whence they came. We can therefore confidently say that our Greek arrived in Africa between October and April. We can say also that the sun's position was as far south below the equator as it could be, being over the tropic of Capricorn on 22nd December, coming back to the equator by about 22nd March, and by 22nd April rising to some eight degrees north of the equator—the equator being the line of latitude on which Mt Kilimanjaro is situated. Now, if we remember the tale 'And Herodotus Said', the sun had changed places in the sky. I am sure our Greek merchant would have noticed and recorded this, but it seems he didn't. Therefore I am left with the feeling that he set forth from

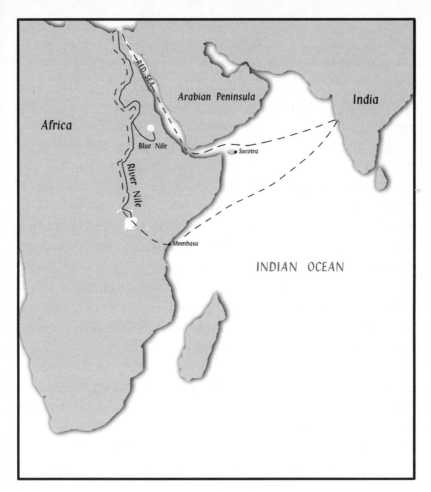

Diogenes' route circa 70 AD _ _ _ _ _ _

India in late March, landed in Africa in early April, and when he set off westwards the sun was back in the northern hemisphere. In this case he wouldn't see the sun pass overhead in a position different from that normally expected in the Mediterranean, because the sun was no longer in the southern hemisphere. As for his journey from India, he wouldn't have noticed anything wrong with the sun's position, because he was travelling south.

I can't say exactly where he landed, but looking at Ptolemy's map you can see he has inserted two islands in the Indian Ocean just off the east coast of Africa. One island is off the Horn of Africa, present day Socotra, while the other is much lower down, and is either Zanzibar or Pemba. If he knew of these, then can we say Diogenes was the person who told him? I would hazard the guess that it was the island of Zanzibar where Diogenes first made land from India. In the sixteenth century, this was where Vasco da Gama found the Arab dhows waiting for the wind to change and take them home with their cargo (which was black and white ivory). It was from Zanzibar that they sailed to the mainland of Africa, although mainly to Mombasa. If Diogenes did travel inland, then he would have been well advised to travel by an easy route—and at that time there was nothing better than a river to guide you through flat or reasonably flat countryside. If we look at our map (a good detailed one, from a well stocked library) we will see a town called Pangani, which lies at the mouth of a river bearing the same name. By following this river, you are heading north west, and will come very near to the base of Mt Kilimanjaro—much nearer in fact than I was when in Tsavo.

Now, our Greek merchant stated that he travelled inland for twenty five days, before coming to the Mountains of the Moon, from which flowed rivers into two lakes. Were those twenty five days the time it took to reach the lakes on the other side of the mountains, or to the mountains themselves? I suspect to the mountains, since the shock of seeing them rising up to the moon would have made an impression deep enough to want to record it. Yet here's an interesting aside. If he was heading for Lake Victoria, he would have bumped into Lakes Natron and Eyasi, which would have funnelled his advance to Victoria. Going through this gap, with Natron to the north, he would still have had another 150 miles to go before reaching Victoria. Ptolemy doesn't show him journeying between the two lakes because, as he was already travelling in a northerly direction, it was only Lake Natron he found, which he went round, and thereafter spun off into the unknown. And I am sure he brought back another legend too—that of the phoenix, the firebird which rises from the flames to live for another 600 years. Today we do indeed have a bird that fits this description, which lives and feeds in great numbers around one lake only—Natron. This soda saturated, steaming lake, situated over one of the earth's volcanic faults, regularly erupts into gushes of scalding water. The birds are the lesser flamingos, whose choice diet of algae colours the plumage a flame red on a white background, not unlike a phoenix risen from the flames. Was it our Diogenes who saw these birds, or disturbed large flocks, and watched as they rose up, as if enflamed from the fires below? I think there is a good possibility that he did.

For our Greek to have got to Kilimanjaro, he would have travelled from the coast directly from, say, Zanzibar—some 200 miles. Some might suggest it was snow capped Mt Kenya he saw, but that would have meant almost 400 miles, and missing Lake Victoria. Had he seen the Ruwenzori mountains, over 700 miles from the coast, he would have seen Victoria before getting there. Anyway apart from all this, he could not have travelled those distances in twenty five days. He would have been on foot, assisted by porters, as was the case with our later, Victorian explorers—and for a very good reason. The region was, until recent times, the home of the tsetse fly, under the impact of which working animals didn't stand much chance of survival. A man could defend himself to some extent—but not a herd of pack animals too. So, in twenty five days, how far did Diogenes get?

Let me now mention Joseph Thompson's expedition, which left Mombasa on 15th March 1883, and arrived in Taveta on 31st March. Most of it was straightforward, until they hit the Taru desert, which *could* have slowed them down, or on the other hand could have spurred them on more quickly, mindful of their water running out. So far they had taken sixteen days. There is an interesting thorn bush which I came across in Tsavo. It's called the 'wait a while' bush, for the simple reason that once you get entangled in it you certainly spend quite some time getting untangled (in fact in the process of trying you generally become more entangled). In other words, this was not country you could travel through with any great speed.

Thompson was a Scottish explorer, and with his dying words, uttered when he was very much older, he said: 'I am not a missionary. I am not an empire builder. I'm not really a scientist. I am just a wanderer.' Yet what a wanderer he was! For a Victorian he'd got unusual flair, *and* a good sense of humour. He carried with him a galvanic battery, which he used to impress the natives, giving them a good jolt of its magical electric shocks. He took a camera to photograph the naked charms of the native girls, and when the elders commanded him to perform some magic to defend them from the Masai cattle stealing raids, he gave them all a drink of fizzing Enos. Of this he has said he could do nothing, yet this was slightly better than nothing.

Thompson was held up in Taveta (approximately 110 miles from Mombasa), because he had heard that the Masai were on the war path. Strange as it might seem, the Masai accepted gifts only such as beads threaded on strings of a certain length, and Thompson was forced to remain in Taveta until he had adjusted 60,000 necklaces. On 18th April he set off and eventually skirted the south west of Kilimanjaro, where he came into contact with a large Masai war party. However, he *was* allowed into their country—although his troubles had only just begun. He was forced to give more and more gifts, and soon found that all his goods were gone. Then he heard that the Masai were planning one of their dreaded dawn attacks.

Quietly, two hours after sunset, Thompson told his men to load up, and they quickly headed back to Taveta, which they reached by 12th May. So here we have a journey that took twenty four days—twelve there and twelve back. He got into Masai country, yes—but the question is, how far? He himself said that he left the forest and at a height of 6,000 ft was in the Masai highland, with a climate reminiscent of Scotland's. Looking at my modern atlas of Africa, I would judge that he got to the highlands between Lakes Natron and Eyasi. So, sixteen days from the coast to Taveta, plus twelve days further inland from Taveta to Masai country, gives us twenty eight— not that much different from the twenty five according to Diogenes.

In any event, it would not have been possible for our Greek to have gone over 700 miles to Mt Ruwenzori in twenty five days, and that is quite apart from the fact that he reached the Mountains of the Moon before the lakes. So, to recap—from the east coast of Africa, he would have come to the lakes *before* Mt Ruwenzori. Mt Kenya would make more sense, *if* he was heading for Egypt, and home, and travelling north. Then he would possibly miss Mt Kilimanjaro, but after Mt Kenya there was only Lake Rudolf—and this would have taken him more than twenty five days. So, I think I'm ahead on that score—though how can I disprove Stanley's claim? Well, quite easily. As I said to my son in law, it's all to do with the way you look at it, or the way Stanley looked at it. Firstly Stanley never saw Mt Kilimanjaro or Mt Kenya. When he saw the snow topped crest of the Ruwenzori ridge, and its mountain, he was coming from the Atlantic coast on the other side of Africa—i.e. the west coast. Like me he could see the similarity between the snow and the moon, although in his case must have been freakishly lucky, since the Ruwenzori mountains are generally covered in rain and mist. Even the local natives had called it 'the place from where the rains came'.

In my opinion Stanley had certainly heard of the legendary Mountains of the Moon, but hadn't heard the story of Diogenes' travels. If he had, he would soon have known he was coming from the wrong direction. His journey from the west had worn him and his expedition out, and had taken nearly six months. Over the Ruwenzori mountains there are rivers that flow into Lake Victoria, and there are lakes as Diogenes stated—but these aren't his Mountains of the Moon.

I am not a scholar, and officially I'm not an explorer—but I do know a man who is—the famous Sir Richard Burton. Burton was the only explorer who equated Kilimanjaro—though he had never seen it—with the Mountains of the Moon. It was on the Speke and Grant expedition of 1861 that Speke first saw Lake Victoria, and considered it one vast lake, whose outlet was the start of the Nile. Unfortunately, he never marched around the lake, or found rivers coming out or going in, but we do now know with hindsight that his assumptions were correct, and that the outlet at the Rippon Falls was the start of the Nile. Now you won't find the Rippon Falls mentioned anywhere except in Alan Moorehead's book *The White Nile*. In it he says, and a plaque was placed at the Falls to say it too: 'Speke discovered this source of the Nile on 28 July 1862.' Yet it hardly matters. The Rippon Falls have now been submerged under a hydro electric dam, and somewhere in the green depths of a river the place where Speke's plaque used to be is obliterated forever. Moreover the Rippon Falls are nowadays known as the Owen Falls Dam. Burton disagreed with Speke, but it was Stanley who confirmed that Speke had been correct.

I have to confess that it does appear it was Stanley who discovered that the greatest river feeding Lake Victoria was the Kagera. Therefore to some degree it could be said that this was the source of the Nile—which is inconveniently west of the lake, and nearer the Ruwenzori mountains. It is this which gave Stanley his reason for saying these were the Mountains of the Moon. Burton didn't lay claim to the Nile's source. But he did link Kilimanjaro with the Mountains of the Moon, and in this observation was on the right side of Africa. When Stanley saw the Ruwenzori range, what he would have seen was the whole ridge as snow capped, with the moon this rendered being an elongated one. When *I* saw *my* moon, it was the crowning pinnacle of one peak alone, a single snow crested cone to that sleeping volcano called Mt Kilimanjaro—a moon in the fullest sense. A moon that our friend Diogenes must have seen as *he* passed Kilimanjaro, before coming to the two great lakes.

Of course, I am biased—but not so biased I would inject words into Ptolemy's pen. He had heard of the tale right enough, and had thought it fit for inclusion in his *Geography*. His detail is extremely accurate. And he could not have shown the Nile doing what it did without someone having passed actual knowledge to him. Likewise Diogenes could not have found the course of the Nile had he simply travelled north from Mombasa via Mt Kenya—a journey of 1,100 miles.

Now who were these people, these explorers? We know about Diogenes. But can we entertain the possibility that some ancient expedition had been initiated at the behest of Pharaoh? Queen Hatshepsut was renowned for sending off expeditions into the unknown. And I am reminded of what Charles Miller said in his book, *The Lunatic Express*—of the legend which places the Masai tribesmen as the descendants of Mark Antony's lost legions. The Masai are a peculiar race. Their features and culture are quite distinct from the other indigenous tribes around Kilimanjaro. Their language is a form of Sudanese from the north, they are tall, slim and sinewy, and they have fine Greek looking faces. No one should ever assume they were weaklings, for they were extremely aggressive, and to quote Charles Miller were the Apaches of Africa. They could run all day without taking a break, they greatly respected courage, and children coming of age were expected to go out and either kill a lion or not return.

Their clothes are also peculiar. Among these is a red mantle (one thinks of a centurion's cloak), which is thrown over the shoulders and resembles a Roman toga. Of course, Mark Antony was a Roman, who had tried to wrest the Roman world from Octavius (later the Roman emperor Augustus). He had joined his legions to Cleopatra's, but had been defeated at the battle of Actium. After that, Antony and Cleopatra took their own lives, and perhaps some of Antony's legions defected to Octavius. There must have been strong supporters of Antony among those legions, men of rank whom Augustus would never have accepted into his army, for fear of revolt. It could just be possible that these marched south to find new lands, driving with them all their wealth in the form of cattle, and eventually, some 1,800 years later, becoming the Masai people. Mark Anthony's demise was before the birth of Ptolemy, and it might be possible that in the early days of his legions' southerly migration, they sent back word of their wanderings.

Although, as Herodotus said, 'Believe it if you want—but I don't!' As for me, I'm open to suggestion.

Thanks to British Airways I can get to Africa in a day, rather than a year, and experience it for myself. It's from that experience that I have come to consider that the ancient Romans had discovered the source of both the Blue and the White Nile, long before slavers or white explorers had penetrated in to the dark continent. Even when those German printers were producing their map, they remembered those earlier historians, who had bothered to set down their discoveries in writing—by which means they come to us, through time and history. So, whoever gave this legend to Ptolemy, in AD150, did so first hand. That I would suggest was no mean feat, and is one we should look on with respect, and with generally a greater reverence than we usually reserve for ancient peoples.

As a parting shot, I shall give you a question to an answer. Is it possible that Ptolemy had got his wording wrong? If you look up to Kilimanjaro, when the sun has set, from your perspective, down in the gloom, is a shadowy staircase rising to the brilliantly lit moon. In reality the snow capped, 20,000 ft volcano should have been named the Mountain *to* the Moon—for that is a truer description. And there's a postscript too, for here is something that has always bothered me. How did Diogenes, who had eventually got to Lake Victoria, know when to head north? In fact why should Diogenes head for the east coast of Africa from India, head westward to his Mountains of the Moon, continue to a vast lake now called Victoria, then find a river running north and decide to follow it for 4,000 miles? He must have followed it into Egypt, since it was he who said that the river from the lake was the start of the Nile.

What bothered me was that evidently he knew when to turn right and head north. It wasn't the lake or the river that made him do that. It was simply that he knew what was the turning point. I looked at my atlas of Africa, and found that the Owen Falls, where the Nile gushes northwards from the lake, is exactly due south of Port Suez. Port Suez gives us a very interesting point, for that, by whatever name it was then known, was a good place to set sail from Egyptian territory if your destination was the Red Sea then India. For this reason I think these ancients knew where in the world they were, north or south of some reference point. They may not have known their exact position, although Diogenes did seem to know that he was due south of his starting point. If he merely gambled in his decision to head north, at just that point where the Nile leaves Lake Victoria, then his odds were extremely long. So how did he do it?

Ptolemy and Eratosthenes, some 270 years before him, had already realised that the earth was a sphere, and had notionally divided it into segments, like those of an orange. This I feel must have something to do with the state of navigational expertise that Diogenes had available to him, and as a great traveller knowledge and skills of this kind would not have been lost on him. It still does though leave the question that if he knew exactly what he was doing, *how* did he know?

That he was using the stars I have no doubt, for it was Zeus who in legend put the Great and Little Bears as constellations in the heavens. Both of these have more or less direct pointers to the Pole Star, and that of course is a sure indication of north. But how did Diogenes know that north was the direction he wanted in order to travel the 4,000 miles to Suez? If the Pole Star was part of his guidance system, then Diogenes must have landed in Africa at a time when the sun was heading back into the northern hemisphere. If the sun had been in the southern hemisphere, below the equator, then he wouldn't have been able to see the Pole Star, and therefore would have found it difficult to determine which way was north. Once the sun had risen, he *could* have identified east, and from that arrived at north. This though is a method that bears a crucial uncertainty, since the sun is continually on the move across the heavens, making it easy to stray off course. The only fixed point of reference is at night, and the Pole Star. Given that, you can place two sticks in the ground making a straight line to it, then in the morning note some feature on the horizon that the sticks are also pointing to, and head towards it. So, finding north in the northern hemisphere isn't difficult, and at the time of Diogenes mathematics and geometry were quite well advanced. Greco Romans could perform an intricate calculation, and by AD80, some ten years after Diogenes, they had built the largest stadium in the world, the Coliseum.

Finding north is one thing, but how did Diogenes know when he was directly south of a desired reference point? This is especially pertinent, since he did move a considerable distance east, to India, then west to Africa, his point of origin being Suez. He then moved west into Africa for at least twenty five days, and seemed to know exactly when he was due south of his place of departure. As we know, the earth is a sphere, and can be viewed as having 360 degrees of longitude. I just cannot believe that out of pure luck he chose the precise degree of longitude as the point to turn north and take him back home, almost 4,000 miles. If there was method in this, then again it would have to be based on the Pole Star, which remains at a fixed point in the sky while the constellations appear to move in a circular motion around it. Diogenes probably also had a timepiece of sorts—

perhaps a sand clock with a twenty four hour cycle. Resetting his clock at midnight, at his place of departure, would tell him, on completing its cycle, when it was midnight again at the place he had left. He would do this in order to get the same alignment of a chosen reference constellation at the same time each day.

I contacted the Greenwich Observatory and spoke to a Mr Harry Ford, curator of the National Maritime Museum. He couldn't confirm my theory, except to say that the ancients had a great deal more ingenuity than we presently know about. He indicated that I was correct in my belief that the constellations rotated once every twenty four hours, but did point out a flaw in my calculations. Because the earth is also moving around the sun, in twenty four hours the earth has changed its position relative to the stars. What this boils down to is an apparent daily rotation of the stars by a factor of 359 rather than 360 degrees. Each day the constellations are a degree out. So, you can see— if you'd departed from your start point 180 days ago, the constellations would be in the opposite position to where you'd expect. Yet here is our Diogenes trotting round the globe! Something tells me these ancient travellers might not have known *where* they were, but they certainly knew how to get back!

You could say that the sailors who took him knew their route there and back. Well, even if they did, where did that leave him once he had entered darkest Africa? In my opinion, he must have had a sophisticated form of navigation, which made me continue to reason it out. The Great Bear and all other stars rotating round the Pole Star will not be in the same position at the same time each night (a good datum is midnight). There will be a shift of one degree per day. We know that Diogenes travelled overland for twenty five days, plus whatever time he took to go from Egypt to India, then back west to Africa. So, unless he understood this one degree error, his direction would be wrong. In just the twenty five days the fault would be twenty five degrees, on the basis of which turning what he thought to be north would put him somewhere in the Indian Ocean.

By AD80 Julius Agricola was conquering the Caledonia of northern Britain. By then most of Britain had been mapped, but it was Julius

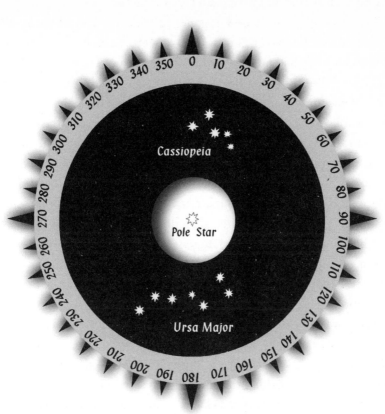

Author's reconstruction of an apparatus that could return travellers from whence they came.

who confirmed that Britain was an island, details he sent back showing a fairly accurate outline of what we know today. I have therefore come to the conclusion that Diogenes knew of the daily one degree movement. After all, observers in his own time would have had ample opportunity to notice that the Great Bear did not come to the exact same spot each succeeding midnight. Zeus or the priests of Zeus had put the two constellations of the Great and Little Bears into the heavens so that sailors could find north at night. The fact that these constellations were there millions of years before man evolved meant that the priests had had time to work them out—and that I think meant they couldn't have missed this one degree variation.

I don't think it could have been luck or the fact that a river ran out of Lake Victoria that made Diogenes turn north. I think he knew when to turn. The river and its course were a coincidence, and in all likelihood he had no idea that it would turn out to be the Nile— that same Nile to the sea through Egypt. He couldn't have known much of the topography in this part of Africa, and for all he knew the river he followed could quite easily have been the source of the Congo. He followed it because it happened to be going in the right direction. It was convenient for water, and for travel—either on or alongside it. It is a fact that wherever rivers are, they generally take the easiest, flattest, and lowest route. I think I can speak for most explorers and say that if you've got to travel, then do so by river—or at the very least beside its banks. When Diogenes did this, he must have been extremely surprised on eventually arriving at Khartoum, in the realisation that here he was back at the fringes of Egyptian or Roman civilisation.

Yet how did he do it? I considered this for some weeks. I am not a scientist but eventually I could see a simple way. Firstly take some vellum or papyrus then make a large circle. Make the circle into a compass rose, by notching the circumference with one degree marks. Then take any one of your marks and divide the circle into four equal sections, by drawing a cross—a red cross. Assuming you're in Alexandria in Egypt, wait until midnight, then take the centre of the cross to be the Pole Star. Take the vertical line through to be your own meridian, and the horizontal line as your horizon. Now insert with dots the position of the stars relative to the Pole Star. From now on, as you travel east or west, record the number of days you are away. Each evening, when your clock runs out of sand, reset it. You now decide to come home and head back west. Each night as you turn the clock you rotate your star chart one degree for every day you've been away. The upright of your cross will no longer be vertical. You now hold your chart to the heavens, with the centre on the Pole Star. Do the constellations match up? If they don't, then continue going west. Continue to do this, moving the star chart one degree for each new day. One night when you hold it up, it will match the stars in the sky.

1 *The four Anubi in Inherkhau's tomb; it appears to be one dog with three heads.*

2 & 3 The place of perpetual music and merriment — Inherkhau's tomb.

4 *Above: The vast crater of Santorini.*

5 *Left: Minoan goddess with upraised arms.*

6 *Below: Unusual stonework on Hadrian's Wall.*

This is when you're directly south of the place you started. It won't tell you *where* exactly, or how *far* south you are—but it will be due south. If you knew the size of the earth, then you could take an angle between the stars and horizon, which would give you an idea of distance. Unfortunately, by Ptolemy's time, the theory put forward by Eratosthenes had already been lost, and Ptolemy's world was only two thirds the size of ours.

It must have come as quite a shock to our Diogenes, as he gazed into the heavens, because at the equator the Pole Star would have sat directly on the horizon on 22nd March. Before March he wouldn't have seen the Pole Star at all. Moreover Diogenes wouldn't have known that it was the earth that orbits the sun. To me this indicates that Diogenes got to Africa in late April, when the sun had already passed the equator, and was heading northwards towards the tropic of Cancer (which it would reach on 22nd June). Even then, with the Pole Star just above the horizon, he could only have matched the top half of his star chart. One can imagine him, sitting at his camp fire trying to puzzle this out. Were there other Greeks in his company, as perplexed as he? And what were the native porters thinking of him—that perhaps it was time to cut and run? To all intents and purposes, Diogenes was indeed sitting on the moon!

I decided to write to Patrick Moore, author of books on astronomy, and for many years presenter of the television programme *The Sky at Night*. I asked him what he thought of my vellum or papyrus star chart. Some weeks later I received a brief postcard that read *Many thanks. Ingenious! Can't see why it wouldn't work*. I can't see why it shouldn't work, either—but perhaps there is someone able to come up with a better and simpler idea. My own is not a complicated method of calculation, though the sand clock would have been a big piece of equipment. That apart, now that we have entered our brand new millennium, I would urge that we think of our ancestors as a great deal more resourceful in their efforts to navigate than hitherto we have been willing to allow. Diogenes was far too clever to enter darkest Africa, almost 2,000 years before our great Victorian explorers, on a chance or hit and miss basis. He knew exactly what he was doing.

Does Merlin Live?

*A*re you sitting comfortably? For then we can begin. Close your eyes and listen very carefully, for I have summoned the wind to take us back almost to the start of this island's history. A time when men who were mighty and renowned walked this land of ours. Men who are now no more than dust returned to earth—yet men who do not die. The embers of their passing still give out warmth. All we must do is blow on the coals, and they will brighten again—and perhaps, if you truly understand, they will burst before our eyes in an eternal flame of life.

It was in the year of Our Lord 43 that the Romans came for a second time to our island—this time to conquer it, and to bring the barbarian tribes of Albion (as it was then known) under the protection of the greatest empire the world had ever seen. It wasn't necessarily a cruel or a bad empire, but it *was* a strong empire. It brought good laws for all men, not just for the rich but also for the poor. It imposed organisation on the chaos of the many small tribes perpetually fighting other small tribes. It brought peace, the peace of Rome, or *pax Romanus*. It brought the inception of towns, markets, straight roads, flush toilets, good sanitation, medicine and health care, simple science, religious tolerance, and a novelty called the baths, where people washed daily. In return it asked for loyalty to the emperor and to Rome.

The Romans were to stay for nearly 400 years. There was not always peace, but in general people prospered and lived longer. Slowly they became proud and happy to be called Roman citizens. But as is the way of things, men strove for power. Some even strove to be emperors, and the empire's biggest downfall lay with these, who often found that they in turn had to fight some new man in order to cling to power. Luckily for this tiny island, lying at the edge of the known world, and now called Britannia, its inhabitants were generally well away from all the problems of civil war. Yet as those 400 years slipped by, instead of preserving all that was good, a certain army officer decided he stood a chance of becoming emperor himself, provided he took his three great legions over to France, which was then called Gaul, to fight for the imperial throne. Sadly he and his legions never came back, but in doing what he did, he had removed all the soldiers who until then had defended Britannia.

Each legion consisted of 5,000 well trained soldiers, and 5,000 auxiliaries. Auxiliaries did the real fighting, while the others looked on. Once they had fought all day, and softened up the enemy, the trumpets blew—signal for the legions to tighten their harness and march forward into the attack. Few if any of the exhausted enemy could ever get to grips with these, an elite among an elite, although now in civil war it had become a matter of legion fighting legion. Britain was denuded of her defences, while its soldiers, with the daily discipline of twenty five years of service, couldn't be quickly replaced by newly trained men. To make matters worse, the following year saw the great winter in Europe, so cold that the Rhine, which flows through Germany (and was the natural frontier between the Roman empire on the one hand and the hordes of barbaric tribesmen on the other), froze over. The barbarians now had a route in, and came with a rush, and in their thousands, howling and galloping over the thick layer of ice. The Romans, having just fought a civil war against the British, were severely weakened. They still had their legions on the Rhine frontier, but like all armies of that time, they were—with winter coming— about to settle into warm cosy quarters until the spring, or the month of March (appropriately named after Mars, the god of war). It was only ever at this point in the year that they would march out and actively patrol and protect the empire. Consequently they were ill prepared for the onslaught they received, in the dead of winter, at the hands of so many hardy warriors from distant northern lands—and so began the slow destruction of a once great empire. By spring the barbarians were well behind the defensive fortifications, pillaging a soft unprotected under belly. They lived in the saddle, eating off the land and following the wind.

Meanwhile, back in Britain, the Saxons had commenced their spring raids, and where there had once been an army to push them back, they now had a free run. To make matters worse, the weak Roman leaders had decided on a cunning but risky strategy. Why not, they reasoned, employ other Saxons as mercenaries, to operate from Britain in repelling their kinsmen? A deal was struck, whereby Britain would pay for two war bands—those of Hengist and Horsa—who would not only be paid, but would receive land for themselves and their families in Kent. (Today there are two ferries which ply the Channel from Dover to Calais—the *Hengist* and the *Horsa*.) Towns on the east coast had already been walled to deter invaders, but now were manned by their inhabitants, including boys and even old men. Not surprisingly, once Hengist and Horsa had landed, and bolstered themselves along the Kent coast, they persuaded their kinsfolk to come and join them— so that now, with a strong and unopposed base, they were impossible to throw back. Civic dignitaries appealed to Rome for help, without success. In fact it came as quite a shock—the people of Britain having enjoyed 400 years of stability—when a letter from the emperor Honorius said that no soldiers could be sent, and that the people must look to their own defences. The people now knew they were on their own.

Greed and a reign of fear now got the upper hand. As each newly successful warrior proclaimed himself emperor of Britain, someone killed him, and usurped his throne—only himself to be murdered. Some of the major settlements were as follows: Colchester, London, Gloucester, Worcester, Chichester, Chester, Cirencester, Ilchester, Lincoln, York, Bath. What naturally followed here was a tendency to close the city gates and establish an army in the role of defence—not only from raiding Saxons, but from fellow countrymen too. While this was going on, yet more Saxons were landing, no longer content to steal and pillage and return to the sea, but intending to stay. Slowly they overran the cities in the east and set up kingdoms that still bear their names today. For example Middlesex was host to the middle Saxons. The east Saxons were Essex, and the west Wessex. Norfolk means north folk, while Suffolk means south folk.

Predictably, a city was conquered now and then, and the Roman Britons heard no more news of it. People fled from the east, burying their valuables as they left (which is why we still keep finding treasure in the eastern counties)—for even then they still believed they would one day return. Occasionally someone did try to organise everyone else to join forces for the common good, though winning the trust of other petty kings proved almost impossible. Roman roads were still in good order, some baths still worked, but the craftsmen had gone and houses either fell into disrepair or were only ever makeshift. The discipline, loyalty and quality of the Roman legions no longer existed, and the skills and knowledge requisite for the training of soldiers was beginning to be lost. It was in these general conditions that Ambrose (Ambrosius Aurelius) found his place in history, for already the shadows had begun to fall that would thicken to the Dark Ages—a time when education and literacy all but ceased, and when recorded history was merely sporadic. That gave rise to myth and legend, though the heroes who were sung—whom I shall sing too—I don't doubt did once live.

Whether the legend of Arthur and Merlin is true or not, one cannot say, but something here did happen. The veil of darkness that was about to fall on the world was for a while resisted—which allowed time and scope for this wonderful story to be passed from father to son. Legend had it that Ambrosius, who was the last leader of the British, fathered a boy. In large part he seems to have been away fighting, and it is possible he never knew about his son. It is also possible he wasn't married. However, that the mother of his child was a great lady, and that Ambrosius was a great leader, there is little doubt. With that as his pedigree the boy was brought up.

Now, it wasn't by any means an easy life for Arthur—although Arthur wouldn't have been his name. This of course is the one that has come down to us, although it is thought he was actually called Artois, meaning Bear. We do have a good idea of this as a sobriquet, because in Bede's *Anglo Saxon Chronicles*—an early history of Angle Land—we may read of battles won by the Britons under the leadership 'of he who is known as the Bear'.

Over the centuries, legend wrought its transformations, so that Artois became Artor, and later Arthur. (One shouldn't forget that it was the Saxons who had been the victorious people, and that it's largely through them—and in part through the Welsh—that some of our history has been received.) In his youth Arthur didn't particularly distinguish himself, and was probably adopted into the household of a minor warlord. It appears he was kept from the fighting, and lived somewhere west of Bath. Before his military training began, he would have been looking after sheep and cattle in the pastures, which were always under threat of raiders. Sometimes this meant the Irish, who in this respect were not without blemish.

It is tempting to think that it was around this time that Merlin appeared, and that Merlin knew all along that Arthur was the surviving son of the last of the Romans. Perhaps he felt that as the only person left with blue blood in his veins, it would inevitably fall to Arthur to unite the Britons and push back the barbarian invasion, which was slowly eating into more and more territory. Who then *was* Merlin? According to legend, he was a wizard, a weaver of spells and magic. That would have been an obvious assessment from a simple, illiterate people, for already, in the year AD520, many of the skills of Rome had evaporated. If Merlin in reality was old—which would certainly confer some of the traditional characteristics of a wizard—then he was possibly among the very last remaining persons of any education—i.e. well read and wise and knowledgeable as to the ways of the world. The ability to read and write might well be taken as absorption in magic, and what it was Merlin got from his books he could no doubt pass on to Arthur. Perhaps it was here on the hillside that Merlin held his class and bit by bit granted Arthur the wisdom that would eventually put them both into history and legend.

As the years passed, slowly the invaders pushed westward. Towns and cities were overrun in their relentless pursuit. Each year travellers brought only news that such and such a town existed no more. As they were conquered they fell into ruin, for the Saxons weren't themselves town dwellers, preferring instead to make clearings in the forest and set up their individual, secluded farmsteads (these were called leys, and if you look on a map they are still to be found. There is an interesting one called Ugley—the clearing of Ug). Archaeologists have identified many of these dying towns, and can tell us of their final hours, when life for the Roman Britons ceased to exist. Yet even in this, there was still a light on the old civilisation—albeit only little—which with Merlin's help flamed up briefly and was bright again.

In the legend there was of course the magic sword called Excalibur, which was firmly fixed in a rock. No one seemed able to pull it out—which was important, since the person who could do so was destined to be king of the Britons. Now in truth this wasn't a sword. The sword was simply a symbol, meaning he who had learned statecraft, diplomacy, leadership, had a brave heart, was resolute of spirit, and could bond people to him—above all he who had the right blood in his veins—was a man of destiny. Arthur did have all these things—which in no small measure was due to Merlin's teaching. Merlin was a truthful, honest advisor who could guide him sensibly—who could, figuratively, cast spells, work magic, bring victory and see into the future. Given these advantages, it isn't too surprising that Arthur would in time wield power of his own, and in a sense wave that mythical sword on high, his people rallying to him.

Even though Arthur may have earned the respect of some or all the jealous lords—even brought them together under one leadership and called himself king—getting them to make their soldiers available to him was quite another matter. In fact this wasn't at all easy. Arthur went from town to city, spreading his word, evangelising, trying to unite his countrymen. His simple message was this—that no longer should each city look after itself alone, but should combine its forces with those of others in order to defeat the common foe. It is likely that the lords and their eldest sons at first refused to give any help. In that case Arthur could have appealed to all second sons—those unlikely to inherit a share in their fathers' estates. After all, they had nothing to lose, and like the crusading knights of the twelfth century, it was they who left home and hearth to acquire property and lands for themselves—or die in the attempt. Perhaps in so doing, in striking out as Arthur's horsemen, one or two soldiers went with them.

Now it was that Arthur called on the knowledge Merlin had given him. Slightly before and during this time, the Roman cavalry had become more heavily protected—not with the plate armour of the Middle Ages, but with scale armour, which still required large and well boned horses to bear it. Legend has it Arthur sent out men to Narbonne in Gaul, to purchase such animals, and that at the same time Merlin taught his smiths to make and thread the scales into suits of war. By then it must have been the case that Arthur's fame was spreading, to the point where landless refugees, with nowhere to go, and not many prospects, marched to join his ranks—old and young men alike, with battered helmets, rusty swords bequeathed by some long dead ancestor who had once served in those mighty legions. Whatever may have been, all these people marched day and night towards South Cadbury Hill, an ancient hill fort now refurbished with steep ditches and newly hewn ramparts of timber—for South Cadbury Hill is what scholars seem to agree was the mythical Camelot of King Arthur.

The might of the legions had gone, and would never return—but the memory lingered. One imagines these sod busters sitting by their fires at night, telling many a tall tale of what they would do when it was time to join battle. Here once again Merlin's guiding spirit would come to the fore, from the books he had read on the arts of Roman warfare. Training techniques, marching order, the wheeling of infantry, transmission of messages by trumpet calls, the stop, the charge, the retire, the use of reserves, the logistics of feeding an army on the move, care for the wounded, burial of the dead, above all how to maintain discipline—these were the crafts he would teach. For a real fighting force, he would add to all that the instant ability to distinguish friend from foe, your place in the line of battle, recognition of the standards of legions and cohorts (one standard has survived to this day, with the dragon flag of Wales). This wasn't trivial, since the standard too was a weapon of war. Archaeologists have discovered a number of these in the form of metal dragon heads that were mounted on a pole and held against the wind. In the dragon's mouth was a clapper contraption that when it vibrated produced a moan or roar, depending on wind speed. On the open end behind the outstretched neck there were hooks, to which would be attached a long and brightly coloured wind sock, made of cloth. To the barbarian enemy, it must have seemed that the army awaiting them did so under the protection of fearsome dragons flying over their heads, roaring and swishing their tails. The poles upholding them would be seen as leashes, temporarily holding them in check.

So the training began, as did the moaning (as modern recruits will tell you), but a strength and a purpose were developed. With the arrival of March they set off eastward to the enemy, and straight into legend. Arthur would have been wise enough always to outnumber the enemy, since he had had to build into his force the notion of invincibility. He, or Merlin, or both of them knew that one day their troops must hold their ground against a larger force than they. Then would their inner strength bear fruit, as Rome had discovered in the past, when her own disciplined legions had stood up against and held at bay greater forces than their own, and won. To us, Arthur's battles are known through Bede's *Anglo Saxon Chronicles*, which I have already referred to. From that source it would seem that Arthur marched his men from one end of Britain to the other, even to the wall of Hadrian. Everywhere he went, Arthur threw the Saxons into disorder, and for a while the Saxon advance west ground to a halt—a time to consolidate. Here, if you possess a map of the West Country, have a look for Wansdyke, a ditch fifteen miles long which runs from west to east just south of Marlborough. It does still exist, but is shallower than in its youth, and this it is that is thought to be Arthurian—a defence system on a much smaller scale to Hadrian's wall, but still requiring considerable effort to overcome. An effort only a strong warlord could command.

Walls only encourage timidity. The only wall that will stop invaders is the wall of human flesh, direct conflict, hand to hand fighting, man to man—no stint on courage. Perhaps, as scholars believe, Arthur needed time—perhaps he couldn't breed horses fast enough to cover his battle losses. Perhaps his mobility was waning, or perhaps he was forced onto the defensive as that began to diminish. To this end, all along the Ridgeway, ancient Iron Age forts, which the Romans had conquered in AD43, were refurbished and newly fortified, thus after years of waste witnessing again the hustle and bustle of everyday military life.

While Arthur was thus consolidating the west, the Saxons had reached a fever pitch of frustration. King Arthur had succeeded when *they* couldn't unite, but now at last a hero did step forward from the ranks—a man all agreed should be leader, or Bretwalda, or king. The Saxons surged forward again, as no small war band, but in their thousands, all eager for glory in battle. Meanwhile, after his military life, Arthur (no more than a mortal man) lapsed into easier ways of life. Did he marry? This I cannot say, but as to the question were there women, I think we can say yes. Women love a hero, and men tend to love women. In my view—and history will bear me out on this— when a man starts to think about women, his brain deserts him. I'm sure that this explains Arthur's internal strife, just as I suspect that now that the danger had seemed to pass, those who were once loyal began to plot against him, with the stage set for a new king to emerge. In legend this was Arthur's period of strife and self indulgence, which he sought to traverse through giving his knights something to do to keep them out of mischief. Here the wily King Arthur fabricated the myth of the Holy Grail, the search for which he sold as none other than a search for the soul's redemption (those who wouldn't embark on this were thereby isolated as truly his enemies).

It was possibly while Arthur's knights were on this quest that the Saxons struck, word of which would take some time to reach them. For a while the Saxons wreaked havoc, and again brought ruin on the land, undoing all the good that Arthur had done. Fortunately his war horses were still intact, but there was no room for further loss. Combat had become difficult, because by now those long fluttering moaning dragon standards held no fear for the enemy, and the Saxons had learned only too well how to grasp a horse's tail and quickly hamstring its rear legs. Perhaps it was now, with Arthur on the defensive, that work commenced on the Wansdyke. According to Bede, many battles were fought in proximity to all those forts along the Ridgeway—hard battles, all closely run. Was Merlin still there, able to guide and advise? Possibly not, for songs and stories have it that Arthur went into the forest at night to call on his old teacher, but without success. Merlin it seemed had returned to the sod from whence he sprang, or was he in his crystal cave contemplating his own eternity?

The Saxons came repeatedly. Arthur threw them back, bloodied and bruised, and made them lick their wounds (and at the same time contemplate the future). For a while a fragile peace did come about— but it was only fragile. A leader can hold his place only on the back of successive victories, and perhaps our Saxon Bretwalda was about to be toppled, or a new one raised up on the shields of the army. Whichever it was, they came again, to the battle of Mt Badon, which we know about, if not its exact location. It signalled not the end as such, but the beginning of the end, for although Arthur was victorious, it was at too high a price. His horses were annihilated, and he himself was mortally wounded, yet was wise enough to know that he mustn't be seen to have died. Like Merlin, Arthur must live forever.

He was laid on his barge and rowed to the distant and mythical Avalon. As for Excalibur, Arthur we are told gave instructions to Sir Bedivere to throw it in the lake. This was a mythical sword that signified power, and I suggest that by this gesture Arthur is telling us there was no one left capable of leading his men. It would mean that even Sir Bedivere himself, no doubt a strong and trusted warrior, wasn't perceived as sufficiently accomplished in matters of statecraft, and couldn't reach a consensus among the lords. By casting away the sword, the question of leadership was open, until someone with the right distribution of gifts would one day announce himself, and pull the nation together. So it was that the legend gathered stuff and weave of its own, and bequeathed to us, and to any future conqueror, an Arthur who only slumbered, who with his knights would eventually stir himself, and girding the harness of war would ride out joyfully to battle, singing his battle hymn—just as in the days of their youth. Youth—when ambition isn't tainted by the spoils and lust for power, which too often arrive with middle age.

Sometimes we think these legends can't have much of an influence on the world and its reality. Yet then we may remind ourselves of a more recent time, when these our blessed isles, set in their silver sea, faced another state of peril. Arthur it was who rose up again, now armed with thunder and clad with wings—for he comes in many guises. Paradoxically our enemies during the Second World War belonged themselves to that same stock of ancient Saxons, and it was Winston Leonard Spencer Churchill—a failure in his father's eyes—who betook to himself the sword of Arthur, and in like fashion cut a swathe through the dark night about to descend on a new and terrible Europe. Did Churchill know and understand his Arthur? It seems impertinent to ask, for how could the author of *A History of the English speaking Peoples* (1956 8) *not* know? I find it hard to keep a tear from my eye, for Churchill, in passing through our eternity, paused, and like the Bear lit the torch of purest knighthood, to illumine the way for succeeding generations. I suspect that, like King Arthur, and with tongue in cheek, Churchill knew precisely the significance of asking to be interred at Bladon (as an echo of that last battle at Badon). If Badon we can't locate, Bladon we can—a village near the Churchill estates at Woodstock, north of Oxford. Do go and visit—he would very much like to see you.

As for Merlin, is *he* dead? I think not. He sleeps in his fairy cave, and waits. For thirteen winters and more he has watched over the child who is now changing to adulthood. At last the thirteenth year is here, and it's the twilight preceding dawn, and a midsummer morning. The child has been told what to say and do—that is, awaken early and go with Grandfather up to the hill where the sheep and cattle pasture. There they sit looking east, where the dawn will bring a new and important day. They watch the second star to the right as the sun rises into a clear blue sky, dispelling the mists of time and youth. On that dawning the child must summon Merlin once more.

For Merlin never dies. He is always here—the bringer of wisdom, knowledge and understanding—gifts to dispel your fears. Perhaps like Merlin you too will one day be old and wise, serene of air and of judgement sound. You, who have seen the creatures of the land, and the air, and that swim in the sea. Who have felt the wind that blows, and the sun that shines, and the rain that falls. Who have seen the grass grow (so seldom greener on the other side), and who have known too the greed, the deceits, and the follies of man. And have there not been kindnesses, and loyalty, and compassion, and the love of those you still call brother? For in all this you have surely understood the lessons of the past, and can behold the future as a door that is merely ajar. Knock, and it will be opened to you—for now is the time to take your grandchild up to that hilltop, and on a magical day watch for the sun to rise.

Merlin, come back. The child must cry but there is no one there, only comforting Grandfather, who will smile down and say: 'You called me, and I am here. Now I can begin, as I have done so many times before.'

Merlin is always here. When he has gone on that long journey into the earth, remember where in the earth he went. Then you can revisit time and again—call out—bid his return—ask comfort—seek help and take his advice…

What Use the Pyramids?

So you thought the pyramids were tombs for the early pharaohs! Well you were right—though in my view the living gods' last resting place was incidental, and not the prime reason these great monuments were built. People have for centuries put forward complicated theories as to why they were constructed—some even suggest the Egyptians were in contact with aliens from a distant galaxy. If that is so, whatever happened to their channels of communication? (Unless by this is meant simply *gazing* at the stars.)

In an approach to the mystery, one has to try to imagine the living conditions of the Egyptians of that time. In those days, religion was extremely important to an isolated people—a people with few foreign enemies. This was mainly because the transportation of water over desert terrain hadn't been fully worked out—naturally a check on any large army—and since Egypt is bordered on three sides by desert, and on the fourth by the Mediterranean, the country enjoyed a long period of stability and relative tranquillity, steeped in its religious rites. Egypt has certain other peculiarities. Apart from the delta region, it is inhabited only along the Nile. Wherever the Nile floods, there is greenery. Almost as if marked off—by the single incision of a knife blade in the sand—the desert begins just three inches higher than the water line, and stretches out hot and humming to the horizon and beyond.

At the best of times, Egypt supports habitation no more than one mile each side of the river—sometimes it is only yards. The Nile, as I have mentioned elsewhere, is about 4,000 miles in length. Eight hundred of these run through Egypt, as nothing more (discounting the delta) than a ribbon. Yet it is precisely this ribbon that has made Egypt the bread basket of the Mediterranean, with the annual flooding—in September and October—bringing with it rich sediments to replenish the farmland. That made life easy, for the only seasons that there were, were governed by the flood. There was a winter and a summer, but the heat and the lack of rain made them as almost one. The sowing of seeds just after the flood, and the harvest some months later, could therefore have been the two principal seasons of the year—certainly seasons of work.

What happened to the populace during the rest of the year? There would be fishing, hunting, and the playing of games. All these we know from archaeological evidence. In later Egyptian history there would have been tomb robbing, but at this stage (c2700BC) there were still serious enough religious observances to make this a forbidden trade. As to war—like necessity a mother of invention—there was practically none (just a few minor skirmishes here and there in the provinces—nothing major). Almost a thousand years would pass before the Egyptians encountered a major invading force, the Hyksos, who brought with them the horse and chariot, in combination a fearsome weapon which the Egyptians quickly adopted.

As for the pyramids, the great ones are at Giza, which we see on postcards (wishing you were here). Dated c2500BC, these colossal monuments are virtually at the end of Egypt's pyramid building era. There were others, of about 700BC, built by the Ethiopian pharaohs, but these were on a much smaller scale. Pyramids had been built about 500 years prior to the great ones of Giza, but at a time when Egypt was in her infancy, and had just begun to experiment. These were at Saqqarah, and were constructed with mud bricks. Some of these went wrong—as in the case of the so called bent pyramid—and it was several years before they got accustomed to using stone. However, by the time of the great Giza pyramids, the era was over. One can only guess as to why this was, aside from the fact that tombs were no proof against robbers. Perhaps one might surmise that with the Hyksos invasion, in 1700BC, the Egyptians lost their opportunity to carry out any large scale project. This would confirm pyramid building in a time span where Egypt had no invaders, and could call on an abundance of labour not otherwise occupied.

What were the alternatives, in times of peace and prosperity? One envisages peasants with nothing to do all day, but moan or bitch or steal, or pick a fight to relieve the monotony. Not even shopping was possible, in the sense that we understand it. Inland was only farm country (for a few hundred yards), and the river bank was a place of habitation. On the west side was the start of the land of the dead, for now the deceased were beginning to be ferried this way, for burial if not necessarily for eternal life. Eternal life, up to 2700, was a journey only Pharaoh undertook—with everyone else left behind. Only later was that as a god given right relinquished, and only then to his immediate family. Little by little, his nobles were also granted it, and as the millennia slipped by peasants gained it too (like Charles I, Pharaoh found his entitlements slowly democratised). But if, as I say, in Egypt's early history it was Pharaoh's prerogative only, then he bestowed from the hereafter goodness and kindness on the land and on his people. Even in death he had control, which was exercised through his descendants, supposedly in direct contact with him, via prayer and sacrifice, supervised by the priesthood. If the Egyptian gods did not exist except in thought, who was it *but* the priesthood who built and enhanced religious rites and principles? They were advisors, counsellors to Pharaoh, who by the time of Tutankhamen were applying pressure for change (1,400 years later perhaps, but proof of Pharaoh's gradual erosion of power).

One of the problems in a country long and ribbon like is getting the people to meet and mix—an important factor in the reduction of inbreeding. Even in early nineteenth century Britain, few villages were without a village idiot. With the advent of the railway, and at the cost of a penny, people began to journey down the track, and thereafter spread their seed more widely. Now it is true that Egypt had, metaphorically, her own railway track, in the Nile itself. There was too a free source of power, being the current to take you down river, and a wind that blew constantly south to bring you back up. In fact the hieroglyph for going down the Nile is a boat with its sails down, and upriver a boat with its sails spread. However, though it was possible and opportune to marry girls from other villages, I'm sure it was just far easier to go courting with someone from your own—which in many cases would be a near blood relative.

My simple explanation as to why the pyramids were built is that Pharaoh asked himself why his people were always causing trouble in the lazy season, and why their communities as a whole had more than a fair share of strangely behaved children. The priests would have advised in favour of a tremendous or monumental task, to keep everyone out of mischief, all able bodied men brought together in one place, under one discipline. Such a project might naturally bring with it other advantages. The womenfolk could also be set to work, looking after the men (food, fresh clothes, etc.). The task could involve a celebration of Pharaoh's reputation—a living god—and so keep everyone in awe of him—and it could in less specific terms act as an uplift for everyone's soul. The task they settled on in fact would one day give Egypt eighty per cent of its foreign earned income, from tourism.

Anyone who was in the armed forces will remember 'the bull'—the simple act of polishing boots, that took weeks, scraping broom handles and toilet seats with a razor blade, cutting the grass with your knife and fork. Hundreds of dreary tasks, designed to keep you out of harm's way. A wage of £1.40 or twenty eight shillings per week was enough for only one night out with a girl. Unless there was something to occupy all other free time, there was opportunity to roam and moan and generally get into trouble—the same consideration which I think gave rise to the pyramids.

We tend to think that a large labour force created the pyramids, yet the converse might be the case—that the pyramids created the work force. One can support that view in the light of the great enterprise of the third millennium BC, which year after year brought together all the people of Egypt, from 700 miles of settlements along the river bank. Yet it wasn't all work. The largest force you can imagine, coming together in one place, wasn't necessarily slave labour. Archaeologists have shown that in a division of teams they vied with one another, and graffiti in one pyramid proclaims 'We are Pharaoh's best'—hardly the utterance of slaves. As for those who may have thought it was the Israelites who laboured to build them, it should be pointed out that the pyramids had been gleaming in the sun for some 1,200 years before Joseph went down into Egypt. So we have a picture, Egyptian youth competing with Egyptian manhood, pushing and pulling those great hewn stones, showing off their vitality and vigour to the girls and women bringing water and the midday meal. Perhaps too there was merriment, a great nocturnal jamboree, for Egypt knew all about beer drinking. Do you think it also possible that couples found each other during this time, and quietly slipped off in the night? Was there a good chance that children were so conceived, genetically sound in body and mind?

If you go to Egypt, you will soon appreciate that the ancients could think, reason and arrive at some sensible ideas. For even after the pyramid era came to an end, the coming together, the great assemblies, didn't cease. All over Egypt great monuments were still constructed, but now in temple or mortuary temple projects. The great obelisk at Aswan was a colossal undertaking in its own right—just cutting it out of the rock was a feat in itself. Unfortunately it broke while being worked on (it still lies there today). Nevertheless, consider the effort involved in rolling it from the mountain, dragging it to the river, then loading it onto a ship to take it downstream to Luxor. Whoever was so engaged certainly wouldn't get bored. And I do think also that almost 6,000 years ago, men in Egypt could look up to see what they had achieved, and be proud and fulfilled. When the time came for the Falcon to rise up to the sun, they came to salute his departure. When a young man finally grew old, would he not have taken his grandchildren to this great edifice and said, 'Look! This is what I did for my living God!' For is it not said that it's a happy man who finds a true occupation?

I would have liked to give you a mind boggling theory—something fantastic—the pyramids as ancient launching sites, for things that could fly in space—but I can't. Theories already in circulation are many and varied, and mine is but one of those. I don't insist that you subscribe to it—I merely offer it up as one more flitch for the melting pot.

Living Forever

*T*he ankh, the symbol of life, of living forever, the sign that always followed Pharaoh's name.... Thanks to the pharaohs and to the pyramids, Egypt does exceedingly well from tourism. For let's face it, the pharaohs and the people of ancient Egypt nearly made that living forever thing. They may not live now, but are certainly remembered—and will continue to be so, which is more than we can say for many of us living today.

As a lover of history, I thought how nice it would be to pull the same stunt. If I could help my descendants long after I was dead—if I could plant a seed whose growth would help them along the way—a seed whose fruit was unity, harmony—if I could uphold certain traditions, that they would revere, and respect—then this might bond the family together, and encourage them to work to a common good. I came to this view when we Anglo Saxons had this terrible habit of leaving each to his own, once the family had broken up—whereas Jews, Indians, Eastern peoples stay in touch over the span of all their surviving generations. This is how they so effectively help each other, both in business and in their social or family life.

My first real thoughts about living forever came through telling a lie in order to get my first job. I claimed to be an archaeologist, when in fact a spade was an agrarian instrument I'd never dream of handling. I was believed, and because of this was considered bright, and therefore got the job. At this point I now had to suffer the trials and tribulations of all those many questions on the subject, from my new and curious workmates. If I didn't want to be rumbled, then it was important to find out as much as I could about it at the earliest possible time. This led to one of those quirks of fate that is life changing. I went to my local library in Kidderminster, to do some research, and in so doing found myself talking to a man called Ian Walker, who, miraculously, was the leader of the local archaeological group. Naturally, and with some relief, I volunteered to go on a dig at Wall Town Farm, near Cleobury Mortimer, in Shropshire. This had once been a Roman fort, on the fringes of Roman Britain, before they expanded their rule into Wales. The fort had been abandoned, then refurbished many years later, serving as depot to troops in transit, marching up to the great wall of Hadrian. It was while digging in the defending ditch at the corner of the fort that eventually my trowel struck metal. For two days I'd scratched away at the site, finding nothing. This was just as well, for not being in any way dedicated to the profession—and only here to pick up the jargon in order to impress my boss and my workmates—I had every intention of keeping all the gold and silver I could carry. At this point in my education I didn't for a moment think I'd find anything less. Little did I realise that the odd nail might be treasure, or that pottery was of the utmost importance (for dating purposes, and in analysing the outpost's day to day operations). So, when metal struck metal, I was so taken aback that I shouted: 'Look what I've found!'

I spent the rest of the day biting off my tongue, for I had found a beautifully designed brooch, in bronze. It was corroded but wasn't broken. A brooch in Roman days was the device holding one's clothes together, buttons and zips having yet to be invented. Both men and women wore them, although the fort was largely male dominated. Now came my great awakening. I sat on the grassy bank, eating an ice cream (a van having just driven by, its proprietor hardly believing his luck, twenty odd people sweltering and digging in the heat, a captive clientele). How did my Roman soldier come to lose this very fine, functional ornament, valued at a week's pay? Why was it in the ditch, and so far from the main gate? In fact you couldn't have got any farther from the gate.

Now, I have been in the army, and I know most of the scams going—which must also have gone on then. So here are my thoughts as to how my brooch had come to be found, after some 1,800 years lying in the sod. We will call my soldier Marcus. He has either bribed his garrison commander, and got a day off—or it's his day off anyway. Like most lads he was possibly a virgin soldier, which we all were once—all quite happy to die for our country, but can we please have a bit of that before we go! So, with the testosterone coursing through his veins, he set off to see the village girls in Cleobury Mortimer. Cleobury Mortimer is certainly as old as Domesday, and I'll wager it was there when these cheeky Romans arrived. I think he was having a great deal of fun—time has this very bad habit of rushing by when the going is good. So much so, that perhaps the sun was already down over the horizon when he girded up his loins and headed back for camp. We may suspect he was late, and it was dark. That so, he couldn't walk through the main gate (unless he wanted extra duties), so he headed in the gloom as far from the gate as he could go. There would have been a sentry, but no doubt that was one of his mates. After some round the hand whispers up at the palisade, he persuaded his friend to walk the ramparts somewhere else, and with a rush scampered down the ditch, up the other side, and started to clamber up the turf and over the wooden surround. We know this was possible, because we had found the turf and some of the timber.

It was here he caught his clothes and ripped off the brooch, which fell back and outwards into the ditch below. I think I can even hear him curse, because there was no going back. He could return in the morning and have a look around, but for now he was heading for his bunk, with no one the wiser.

The fort may have been well in from the frontier. Archaeologists have shown that Romans could be just as lazy as the rest of us sometimes are, for they seldom cleaned out their ditches, being galvanised into doing so only when danger was on its way. If this was the case, and the ditch was quite overgrown, then hero Marcus might have looked and looked, but never found his brooch. It was for me, 1,800 years later, to retrieve it.

I was spellbound by what I had done. I had reached back in time and lived out that day again. Like St Paul on the road to Damascus, I had seen the light, and I was now ensnared in a world of history, where mortals had lived, where they seemed to live again, around me everywhere—I could see and feel and hear them. It meant to me that history wasn't so much dust—it lived and breathed.

———————

Now there comes a time in your life when something so tragic occurs you cannot believe it. Your mother dies. (How could she? She was going to live forever.) I was devastated, and the tears ran and ran. Somehow I couldn't quite let her go—in some way she'd got to be remembered. I wrote down everything I knew about her and her family—all that she'd seen from the Kaiser to Adolf. I expressed my love for her, and what a wonderful mother she had been. The tears blotched the ink, but I didn't care. Joyfully I told the future that these where *my* tears, and that the last word I would mumble in this world would be 'Mother'. I then took my letter and placed it in a polyurethane bag, and sucked out the air. I took more bags and inserted her birth, marriage and death certificates. I took also a lock of her hair, photos of her youth, photos with me as a baby, of her marriage, and more recently of her in old age. I even selected a pair of gloves that she'd worn at my wedding. All these I vacuum packed in more polyurethane bags. I then took the lid of a large biscuit tin, and putting that too in polyurethane I poured in plaster of Paris. While still wet I carved an inscription into it (like the commandments in tablets of stone), as to who was within. In it I placed two coins, struck in the years of her birth and death—just in case she had to pay the ferryman. I then took an ordnance survey map of the area showing where she had lived and where she was buried. I made another tablet, and sandwiching my polyurethane bags between them, wrapped them together with bandages, smearing round the edges more plaster of Paris. As a final preservative I deposited this in another large polyurethane bag, vacuumed once again. Armed with my package, I laid it by her side in her coffin.

Even so just before her burial I had to fight with the bureaucracy. My grandparents had died about five years before, and were buried in the same churchyard. All the graves were in a row, one after the other down the field and on the way back up. The next vacant plot—for my mother—was one grave from my grandparents'. (In his lifetime my grandfather had gone to the States looking for work, and had come back with tales of being beaten by the Ku Klux Klan, and shaking hands with Buffalo Bill Cody.) How nice, I thought, it would be, to leave her resting at the feet of her parents.

'Please, Mr Graveyard Man, can I skip a plot and move one up? After all, the locals are popping off like flies, so you'll soon fill it.'

Imagine my amazement when the nice Mr Graveyard Man said, 'No, you've got to take the next vacant one.'

I could hear the distant trumpets blow, the neighing of warhorses, the steady tread of marching feet. 'Hit him one!' cried my legions.

I gave him one of my crooked smiles, for he didn't know he was taking on the Milky Bar Kid.

'You win!' I said, and paid the ferryman his fee of £14 for the plot. He smiled smugly at me and signed the papers.

'Now,' says I, still with my crooked smile, 'I'll buy the next plot for my mother, because this one is for me.'

Luckily for me, he had never heard of cunning Odysseus. I am also pleased to say I haven't yet had to use my plot, whose value is now inflated to £184 (if you're ever in my graveyard, on a dark and windy night, and you see an old man jigging up and down, it's only me, dancing on my grave).

Six months later my father died of a broken heart, and for him too I deposited grave goods. My daughter has been told that I too must go after this fashion, and if environmentally friendly forces persuade her to incinerate me, then my whole estate goes to some lucky dog.

Yet because I have made these arrangements, my parents and I just might be living forever. Eventually the graveyard will be forgotten, and one day perhaps my grave will be turned over to developers, who might just stumble on our bones and our eternal chattels. Then like Ginger in the Egyptian department of the British Museum, my parents and I might once more see the light of day, where school children will come to look and even I hope wonder.

But this won't affect my descendants, who will eventually no longer come to visit—therefore how can I get the memory of us to fasten on to them? How did the nobility manage to instil into *their* unborn descendants a sense of being and family tradition? They didn't have camcorders or even film. They did it by the simple expedient of building stately homes and lining the staircase with portraits of themselves—a staircase little Johnny had to climb each night to his wooden bed. As you can imagine, it wouldn't be long before Johnny might ask, 'Mother, who is that?'—and slowly a sense of being and tradition would make themselves evident. There would be keepsakes brought back from distant times and distant campaigns, each one contributing to the nurture of the child developing into a man, with the process repeated over the next generation. We might think that the nobility are a waste of time and money, but that would be a limiting view. They have had the best education, they are British through and through, and when the time comes to do one's duty, to lead and if necessary to die, they generally do so with a panache I am proud of.

Now, for me, it is nearly time to play the part of Merlin, the eternal grandfather, preparing to teach his grandchildren. Grandfathers are generally better at this than parents. This is mainly because they have not become so familiar, and to some extent are held in awe, if only due to their age. If you're a good grandfather, who can tell a good tale—a tale which bears a seed of truth, is educative, and moral (no mistakes, otherwise you lose credibility)—then you shouldn't have trouble holding their attention. Once upon a time grandparents did play a significant role in family upbringing. Their sons had the strength and the brains, but not the wisdom, and while the sons toiled the grandparents passed on their knowledge—to son, daughter, and to grandchildren. Now we are an affluent society, families have broken up and live miles apart, contact is no longer considered important.

Not being noble, with a long history of illustrious ancestors, and having no stately home to show my worth, what can I do to shape my descendants' upbringing? I can buy a working antique in the shape of a rocking horse—a good one, that can and will be handed down and treasured. I have had made for me a special warhorse, from natural cherry wood, with a flowing mane and flashing eyes. It has blue saddle cloth edged in gold, and a gold star emblazoned on the front to denote leadership. On my magical horse, which is destined to gallop into the future, I have had a brass plaque mounted, whose inscription is as follows:

Though I sleep for many many years,
I shall be
FAITHFUL
from generation unto generation

—and listed too are both mine and my father's name, as the founding fathers, with an exact date.

This steed is now immortal and is setting forth at a gallop, not through distant lands but through time itself. It is the embodiment of me, and through it my family and I stand a good chance of living forever. Naturally I have called it Faithful, and on it have affixed a small silver plaque, showing Oliver Carratu to be the first rider. I like to think that in the distant future it will be emblazoned with many other names, so that each child in turn asks the question, 'Mummy, who were those other children?' Then like Odysseus, and as a final insurance, I have made Faithful into a Trojan horse, for in it is a secret compartment—not to conceal warlike Greeks, but letters of greeting to all those who will come to ride my steed.

What other things could I do, to assist my family? Well, not a lot of people know this, but this granddad is one of the oldest back packers in town. Since my semi retirement I have travelled through India and parts of China. I have also taken as model the book *The Conquest of New Spain* by Bernal Diaz, who in 1518 was a foot soldier of Cortez. I have followed in those footsteps on a journey of conquest of the Aztec empire. Starting where he and his compatriots landed, at Vera Cruz, then marching on to Tlaxcala, to Cholula, I climbed the great pyramid, and heard the church bells ring out. I imagined Cortez's tiny army, marching to their destiny and into the pages of history. From there I went through the Pass of Cortez, with the Volcano of Popocatapetl (the mountain that smokes) on the one side and Ixtaccihuatl (the lady with the white mantle) on the other. I went ever upwards, making use of a bus now and then, to the now polluted city of Tenachtitlan (Mexico City). What a wonder it was, even though I was almost 600 hundred years too late to be one of them, on one of history's greatest adventures.

After the exhilaration of that, I decided to do something similar the following year—to follow Francisco Pizarro and his conquest of the Incas. My daughter gave me a journal, to detail my travels. When I opened it and started to write I was saddened to find it was for pampered tourists, for every other page was for entries on hotel names and star ratings, menus and local restaurants, quality and cost of meals, etc. Now I know a five star hotel in Europe when I see one. I can only say that in comparison what I found ranged between anything from minus ten to minus three, and the food generally consisted of potatoes and corn on the cob, with perhaps some chicken if available. The potatoes and corn were done in many different ways, but hunger and exhaustion make one appreciate anything. However, it did strike my Homeric sense of humour that here was a situation I could use to give my grandson a little perk in life, with the agreement that my journal was only to be given him once I had made the journey over the river Styx.

My honourable ancestors were a strange bunch of labourers (only two could write their names) whom it had taken me a considerable time to find in Somerset House, though I did have great respect for my father, who effectively started our family. He was an orphan, whose own father had happily lied on his wedding day, as to his age, marrying in my grandmother a woman who was nine years his senior. A consequence of this was my trying to find someone who appeared not to have been born.

It was because my father was an orphan that he had taken all the gambles in life—and won. By rights I should have been a labourer, like him and many before him. It is because of this that I see my father as the one who dragged us into the sunlight, and for that I am eternally grateful. But, however much I tried to tell my daughter of this great leap forward, she didn't catch on. She upset me further in giving my grandson four names, not one of which was a family name. I appreciate that that was her choice, and her decision—nevertheless I did feel entitled to be a little put out. So, with the aid of this journal, I conceived a cunning plan, which so to speak would kill *three* birds with one stone.

As I set off on my adventure to Peru I started to write. At Lima I began to take in the sights, before moving inland to the majestic Andes and the heart of the Inca empire at Cuzco. I would record everything I saw, and to round off the day's adventures I would make this entry: 'I am being followed. I know I am being followed. I can't see him, but I know he is there.'

I saw condors, volcanoes, giant cracks in the earth where it was literally opening up. I saw ancient sites and burial grounds which where the wind had blown the sand away revealed mummies long dead. I flew over the Nasca lines, got caught up in an avalanche, swam in hot sulphurous volcanic springs, got cold, got hot, got short of air and chewed coca leaves. I saw vast ancient terraces of land rising high above the clouds, bananas growing on the lower tiers, potatoes on the uppermost (to walk from the bottom of your farm to the top took two days). I saw raging rivers that were tributaries to the Amazon, which still had 3,000 miles to go before coming to the sea. All this I recorded, but each day insisted: 'I am still being followed.'

It was in this way at Machu Picchu, high above the cloud line, that I was occupied with my journal. I looked down into the valley below. There coming toward me was a cloud with all sails set like a stately Spanish galleon. It hit the mountain and started to climb, and in ascending the ruined steps I was seated on, it enveloped me. When such clouds arrive—and they do so regularly—the sun is blotted out, visibility is severely reduced by a thick fog, and it rains. I continued to write—'There is a stranger coming up the steps. I don't recognise him, but I feel this is the man who has been following me. He is old but he has a young boy helping him. I peer at him and then I recognise those eyes. Yes, I do know him! He is my grandson Oliver, and the young man at is side is my great grandson Henry.'

So I finished my journal, but not before informing it that I was leaving a time capsule for my grandson to find. As to what I put in it, that would be telling! And anyway he wouldn't then have to leave his cosy fireside chair. It's enough to say it's a small treasure, which I hope he will one day go and seek. If he can endure the rigours of Peru, then he *will* be the man I hope him to be—someone who is unafraid, who embraces adventure, who is inquisitive and interesting. Perhaps he will recall the respect I had for my father, and repeat it in the respect he shows to me, by giving his son the name Henry. If he does this I can turn over in my grave and sleep a contended sleep, for all will be well with my family.

However, it is not my wish to short change you, for there are some who must have been thinking I am withholding the secret of eternal youth. For myself I plan to live to the age of 104, so that I can watch over and enjoy my descendants growing up. I will willingly impart that knowledge, but it will be up to you to believe in it or not.

Firstly I am lucky to have had an excellent diet during World War II. As a youth, I was pushed into sport and built up a good framework of bone and muscle. On leaving school Her Majesty the Queen desired that I join her armed forces, and to enjoy all the physical exertion that went with that. My brain has always led an active life, learning to fear nothing, not even death itself. Fortunately I had a gene missing too, which caused me—although very sporty myself—to abhor sport from a spectator point of view, which gives me time to broaden my horizons through travel and devouring books. I also realised that what you ate could affect your health, and so refrained from fat and sugar. My brain was in control, and not me, and my body was only there for gathering food to nourish that brain. In return the rest of my time was free. I have always thanked my brain for giving me the right decisions, and reciprocally my brain has thanked my body by keeping it fit and healthy. We live in perfect harmony, and suffer few or no ailments, except the odd broken bone. I drink alcohol and eat meat in moderation. I take food when I feel like it, but I abhor large meals.

That said, I have always pondered why I was getting older, but my brain was staying young, at about twenty. Then I discovered that we don't grow old at all, since our body renews everything on a regular basis. We do however change, and that is simply because our body is, in renewing itself, making a copy, and each time it does this it makes a slight mistake. It may forget to give you a full head of hair or even forget to renew your hair pigment, so we go bald and grey—but we're still young. Contrary to this we are constantly being told that we *are* getting old, and to take it easy. As we're only human, we like to fuss, and so we go along with this. So much so that some of us buy clothes for the older person, because we think we ought to. We might call them sensible but in reality we're trying to look how we think we should look. We don't run or jump or play the fool as we did in our youth, yet if an eighty year old woman can run a marathon, why can't we allow ourselves some licence as to Tom Foolery!

You might ask then that if our bodies remain fresh and new, what causes death? It appears we are like our cars, subject to corrosion. Oxygen in rain water attacks the metal, and iron oxide is formed, which we know to be rust. Rust is not as strong as steel, so we—as with our cars—become 'flaky'. Now within us we have what is known as 'radicals' and 'free radicals'. Radicals are in pairs, like a husband and wife, and go sailing harmlessly round our bodies. The free radical is more the single male. This causes all the problems, because he wants to break up the radicals and team up with one of them. In doing so this causes damage and slight corrosion—if he teams up it leaves one spare, which immediately starts the process again. How can this be cured? It can't, otherwise we *would* live for ever—although we *can* accelerate or retard it.

Free radicals are created by oxygen (which we can't get away from), by smoking, by sunlight, and—so I am informed—by barbecued food. The good news is they can be combated by taking vitamin E, fresh fruit, vegetables, red wine (though beware here—too much can make you depressed), and cranberry juice. Yet this is only the half of it, for the biggest cause of death is letting your brain stagnate. Boredom will kill you quicker than you know—therefore it's important to give yourself something to think about—a new place, with its sights, sounds, its evocative smells, and even its hardships. Don't be frightened of the weather—the rain, wind, snow or heat. Just be pleased with what you get, and remember that there isn't any weather in the grave. The brain will revel in getting you through, and believe me—the brain doesn't want to die, and your legs, arms and eyes are only its servants (you can lose an arm and live, but not your brain).

The idea seems to be that when you retire at sixty five you can expect to live till you're seventy. At least, that is how the pension funds are conceived. It is in those five years that most people numb their brains to submission. Personally I don't go a lot on golf, but when I see my contemporaries waiting for the club to open early in the morning, I wonder what they have to stimulate their lives. The walking is good, but I couldn't get any satisfaction in putting a small ball into a small round hole day after day. The brain was designed for better things than that.

Professor Stephen Hawking, who wrote *A Brief History of Time*, should have been dead years ago, but lives in a wheelchair, with O what a brain! It simply hasn't got time to die, it's enjoying itself so much! So, please, take that as an example—and don't bore yourselves to death.

If you want to live nearly forever, then don't ever think of yourself as old. Ride a bike, climb a mountain, run into town, read books, travel—even if it only means taking a bus to the next town—and don't be frightened of asking why. For this is one of the greatest words we've ever produced. Learn everything this wonderful world has got to teach you, because your mission, in retirement, is that of showing how wise and healthy Granddad and Grandma are.

Your grandchildren will learn from you, for didn't Omar Khayyám once write that there are four types of people in the world:

> There is he that knows not and knows not he knows not,
> he is a fool, shun him;
> There is he who knows not but knows he knows not,
> he is asleep, awaken him;
> There is he who knows but knows not he knows,
> lead him.
> And there is he who knows and knows he knows,
> he is wise, follow him.

The Day Noah Put to Sea

Every religious scholar will tell you that Noah was on a river flood and never did put to sea. Perhaps they, like me, simply cannot conceive of all the waters of the world rising to cover Mt Everest, or even Mt Ararat. According to my calculations—which are generous, I think—if both ice caps melted completely, then the waters of the world would rise some 800 feet. Therefore if Noah *was* in such a flood, he would have risen to an eventual height some 800 feet above his starting position. His horizon would also have done this, doubtless giving to Noah's purview land sticking up *somewhere*.

A puzzle all this might have remained, had not someone, somewhere, written in a book that a certain ancient historian had it that the Jews were exiled from Egypt *because* they were suffering a wasting disease. I would have passed this over, except that the book's author dismissed the very notion as, and I quote, 'frankly...quite ridiculous'. Explaining *why* it was ridiculous was not something it occurred to him to do. At this point my curiosity got the better of me, so, cunningly, I sent off a stamped addressed envelope to the British Library, and asked for information about this ancient explorer. Almost by return of post I was sent a manuscript, which set out the history of the wars of the Jewish revolt, as chronicled by an eminent Roman historian. So, without further ado, I should like to introduce P Cornelius Tacitus, one time soldier, senator, governor of Western Anatolia, and Consul of Rome.

He was born in AD55, and died in 122, and to his readers was known simply as 'Tacitus'. I had met him before, having read his books *The Germania* and *The Agricola*, in which he recorded his father in law's governorship of Britain. Tacitus had also written *The Annals of Imperial Rome* and *The Histories*. I in common with other scholars have found him an accurate and reliable reporter, which isn't to say he couldn't be biased (that's only to be expected). He was strict about detail, enjoyed a good following in his own times, and almost certainly wouldn't have been tolerated if prone to stupid or unsupported comment. Any writer will tell you, there is no lack of persons eager to tear your ideas to shreds.

Now, it is not his fault if he sometimes assumes we should know automatically and precisely what he's referring to. In his own day Rome was the greatest power the world had ever seen, having been established for 500 years and showing every likelihood of lasting to eternity. It should also be remembered that Tacitus would have been too young to write first hand on the Jewish revolt, being about fourteen when Rome decided to step in and give the Jews a thumping. This was under the future emperor Vespasian. Tacitus, if pro Vespasian, was not the first to write on the Jewish wars. It was to Josephus Flavius that that privilege belonged—the so called Jewish traitor.

Josephus (AD37 98) was born Jewish, was well educated, and initially fought against Rome. However, he foresaw the outcome, and the futility of it all, a situation made all the more fragile by the continual bickering of the Jewish leaders. Consequently, and after almost losing his life through these many internal conflicts, he switched sides and threw in his lot with Rome. It is therefore reasonable to deduce that Tacitus' account owes a great deal to what was originally a Jewish source—namely Josephus. Both were in Rome, both were pro Vespasian, and both raised pens on the Jewish question.

Here I was about to relate to you what Tacitus had said, when something bade me 'Hold!' A quiet, yet strong, and no nonsense voice seemed to say, 'Let me come forth. Let me clothe myself in the warm flesh of mortals and leave these cold halls of Hades. Let me dwell once more amongst you.'

Could I steal his thunder! 'So be it, honoured father of Rome. Speak on.'

'EIUSDEM ANTI PRINCIPIO CAESAR TITUS, PERDOMANDAE AIDER DELICACIES A PATRE ET PRIVATIS UTRIUSQUE REBUS MILITIA CLARUS.'

At the beginning of the same year, Titus Caesar had been selected by his father to complete the conquest of Judaea. He had already won a name for himself as a general, when he and Vespasian had the status of subjects. But now his activities received added support and recognition, as provinces and armies vied in displaying their enthusiasm. He was anxious to live up to his new position by cutting a fine figure and showing enterprise in arms. His polite and affable manner gained him devoted followers. In military duties and on the march he often mixed with the ordinary soldiers without sacrificing the respect due to a commanding officer.

Waiting for him in Judaea were the three legions that had long served under Vespasian—the Fifth, Tenth and Fifteenth. To this force must be added the Twelfth from Syria and drafts from the Twenty Second and Third brought up from Alexandria. He was attended by twenty cohorts of allied infantry and eight regiments of cavalry, as well as by the two kings Agrippa and Sohaemus and the supporting forces offered by King Antilochus. Then there were strong levies of Arabs, who felt for the Jews the hatred common between neighbours, and many individual adventurers from Rome and Italy who for various reasons hoped to ingratiate themselves with an Emperor whose ear might still be gained. This then was the army with which Titus entered enemy territory. He advanced in an orderly fashion, maintaining good reconnaissance and a state of readiness for battle, and encamped at no great distance from Jerusalem.

As I am now to record the death agony of a famous city, it seems appropriate to inform the reader of its origin. The Jews are said to have been refugees from the island of Crete, who settled in the remotest corner of Libya in the days when, according to the story, Saturn was driven from his throne by the aggression of Jupiter. This is a deduction, from the name Judaea, by which they became known. The word is to be regarded as a barbarous lengthening of 'Idaei'—the name of the people dwelling around the famous Mt Ida in Crete. A few authorities hold that in the reign of Isis the surplus population of Egypt was evacuated to neighbouring lands under the leadership of Hieroslymus and Judas. Many assure us that the Jews are descended from the Ethiopians who were driven by fear and hatred to emigrate from their home when Cepheus was king. There are some who say that a motley collection of landless Assyrians occupied a part of Egypt, then built cities of their own. Most authorities however agree on the following account:

The whole of Egypt was once plagued by a wasting disease which caused bodily disfigurement. Pharaoh Bocchoris (Tacitus has received the wrong information here, as Pharaoh Bocchoris reigned 721 715BC, by which time the Jews were firmly established in Jerusalem), Bocchoris went to the oracle of Hammon—known today as Ammon or Amon—to ask for a cure, and was told to purify his kingdom by expelling the victims to other lands, since they lay under a divine curse.

Thus a multitude of sufferers were rounded up, herded together and abandoned in the wilderness. Here the exiles tearfully resigned themselves to their fate. One of them, who was called Moses, urged his companions not to wait passively for help from God or man, for both had deserted them. According to Moses, they should trust in their own initiative and do whatever they must to overcome their plight. They agreed and started off at random into the unknown. Exhaustion set in, chiefly through lack of water, such that the plain became strewn with the bodies of those who were at their last gasp. When a herd of wild asses left their pasture and made for the shade of a wooded crag, Moses followed, and so was able to bring to light abundant channels of water whose presence he deduced from a grassy patch of ground. This relieved their thirst and they travelled on for six days without a break. On the seventh they expelled the previous inhabitants of Canaan. Then, in order to secure the allegiance of his people in the future, Moses prescribed a novel religion quite different from those of the rest of mankind.

Tacitus' history goes on in some length but this is the only part of his narrative that we need. So here we have it. Tacitus gives four places for the origin of the Jews, of which two—although spurious—fit perfectly well with the Biblical account: the coming out of Egypt, and the return from exile in Babylon.

What held my attention was this unusual place of Crete during the aggression of Saturn (or Kronos) and Jupiter (Zeus). If the Jews did come from Crete, that same aggressiveness of the gods or God might well have been visited on Noah when the flood was unleashed. If Noah was involved in a river flood, it follows he couldn't have been at sea. Or was he? For Noah was quite adamant that the world, or his world, was completely covered in water, and this might well have been the case, his world being a very small world indeed. Did Noah for example know that the world was round? If so, did he understand horizons? Did he know that passing over the horizon meant seeing the land you'd left behind disappear from view? If he didn't know this, then logic would rather dictate that the land had been engulfed by water. What kind of water – sea or fresh – it is doubtful Noah could have known, being unable to differentiate between the two. Even if for him it may not have been raining at the time, it must have been pouring down somewhere else. Odysseus, of 1200BC, accepted but didn't understand this phenomenon: 'So soon as we sank the Cretan hills and had only sea and sky in view…' (*The Odyssey*, trans T E Lawrence, p149)

To a man unaware that the world was round, there was *no* horizon, so that what he might see in the direction he'd come from was water encroaching on the land. He wouldn't have to go far to observe this—certainly no more than ten miles—provided there was no intervening landmass. Here therefore is a perfectly sensible explanation of what Noah—or the group of people we shall henceforth call Noah—saw and recorded. If Noah was at sea then Noah recorded the truth.

I am further indebted to David Easold and his book *The Discovery of Noah's Ark*. He too falls into this deadly trap, and in his Introduction (pXIV), says, '...and finally, the illogical idea of a flood that could cover the whole world, may be based on memories of a great flood but is certainly a difficult concept for the non believer to accept.' Yet in saying that Easold and many other scholars are quite happy to go searching for the ark in the mountains of Ararat. Ironically, from my simple concept of horizons, and as a 'non believer', I do in fact accept that Noah saw his world disappear below the waters.

However, I did need more to go on than this, and strange as it might appear it was a bird that gave me the clue I was after. Moreover it was a bird I found in the Bible. As it says, 'Noah let fly a black raven and it flew to and fro until the waters of the world abated.' There was of course a dove also, but that he let fly later. The raven came first. Why? Was it because it was big and black? Was it because a raven can't swim, but *can* soar to heights of up to 17,000 feet (and more if it must)? One must add to this that a large black bird can be picked out easily against the blue of the sky from the deck of a ship, which could be a navigational boon if that ship is none too sure in which direction land lies.

I am therefore asking was the raven used as a navigational instrument. The compass and the compass rose, with a complete 360 degrees, was still in the future. The only aid sailors could rely on was the position of the sun at sunrise, which we now call east. It was only later that they worked out how to use the stars. Having pinpointed east, the other cardinal points could only be approximated, though of course once the sun was up, there was little more to go on. In short if a crew was heading eastwards from Crete and needed to make landfall in Cyprus to replenish water and supplies, it could never be determined until land was sighted whether or not position was too far north or too far south. It is very likely then that in such cases the sailors would release their on board raven, which having flown high enough to see well over the horizon would sight land and make its direct flight to *terra firma*.

The raven is the largest of the crow family, and for generations the crow's nest has been an integral part of the ship—the very name rebounds throughout folklore. And what a strange name it is for a lookout point, yet not so strange if that was the place you kept your crow. We also talk of the shortest distance between two points as being 'as the crow flies'. Yet over land the crow doesn't behave like this. It flies whither it wants, winging over fields and hedgerows as the whim takes it. Over sea, however, it's a different matter, because in those circumstances the crow will always fly in a straight line towards nearest land. Therefore that terminology which we still tend to use could only apply to a crow cast out at sea. As far as our ancient mariners were concerned, once they saw their raven settle on a direction and fly, then it was simply a matter of helm hard over and follow behind. As they came over the horizon, land would appear just as if the waters were abating, making our bird, our raven, the first recording of a ship to shore instrument of navigation.

We know that Cook and Columbus looked for birds in the sky as a sign that land was nearby. I am reminded of U boats in World War II, tracking enemy shipping. The secret was to tow a small one seater gyroplane, which rose to some height in order to yield a better and distant view. If you were a really clever sailor what about collecting a few birds in a cage and taking them with you? Then if you were lost you let loose the biggest, strongest, blackest—like Alexander the Great, who when lost in the Egyptian desert, and looking for the oasis of Siwi, was saved when he followed the birds back to the water hole on their nightly return.

Now, the trouble I have had with research of this nature is that once I think I've discovered all that there is to discover, something more turns up. I owe something to the saga of Floki Rogaland, a Viking of circa AD815, who set forth from the Faeroe Isles to discover new lands to the west. Lost on the storm tossed Atlantic, he eventually released two ravens and noted which way they flew. I feel I can understand his apprehension. He was in a bad way, and to release those birds was a very big gamble, particularly when it's doubtful there were that many birds on board. Every time you let one go, you were losing a lifeline. To let two go might be considered rash, though I imagine they were released at intervals. Perhaps the first one got lost, or following its flight afforded no swift result. With what sighs of relief the second (and possibly the last) gave better results, when the clear view of a shoreline turned out to be that of Iceland.

What is notable about Noah and the raven is the impression it so obviously left on him. He was astounded, and that was because when the bird flew away it wasn't long before land rose up from the waters. Gibbon points out in his *Decline and Fall of the Roman Empire* that there are no camels in the Koran, and that is perhaps because, to its writers, camels were so commonplace that they hardly rated a mention. We never think to relate the blindingly obvious, so it is therefore a fair guess that to Noah this technique with the ravens was so unfamiliar as to be worth his while noting it. This rather implies that it was someone other than Noah himself who released the bird—some expert who'd done it all his seafaring life—or the ship's captain. If we can come to that conclusion, then we might also say that Noah rather than *build* his ark *chartered* it. If then we can still consider that Noah was involved in a river flood, then the raven becomes illogical—there was no reason for a river craft to have such a bird. The crew would always know where the river bank was, even during the greatest river flood—that's to say parallel with the flow of the water.

It is interesting to note that the raven didn't come back to the ark—so what was its fate? Did it drown? I think probably not. As Noah said, the waters of the world abated. When he released the dove, it couldn't find land to rest its feet upon. So here there would appear to be a contradiction. In my view, Noah is recording faithfully what he saw—that is, two types of bird used as a navigational aid. Again I am opening a door for future archaeologists and historians, for I think the use of these birds was standard practice to Minoan sailors of that period. I consider that the practice was continued right through the history of seafaring folk in the Mediterranean, until the invention of the compass—a practice so familiar that like camels to the Koran writers, it scarcely rates a mention. When one considers that the Minoans traded all around the Mediterranean, one has to ask by what method they found Malta, a mere dot in the sea—which is very easy to miss when travelling west. Our raven is so convincing an explanation it would be foolish to ignore it.

But what about the dove? Incidentally the Bible makes no mention of its being white—that's something we've added in order to reinforce its symbolic association with peace. In any event, either a white or a grey dove would not have been easily identifiable against a blue sky. Yet we do know that the dove was used as a messenger, even if the message it carried was only in the form of an olive leaf (a sign, as we know, speaking volumes—in fact the symbol of peace). Why should the dove mean peace to Noah? Surely the olive leaf was meant to convey the message that the waters were drying up and life was returning to the earth. In Genesis (8: 8), 'he sent forth a dove from him, to see if the waters were abated from off the face of the ground'. He states that he let fly three doves at seven day intervals. One returned empty handed. The second returned with a plucked olive leaf, while the third returned not at all.

We all know that pigeons and doves are of the same family, and that they have great homing abilities. What if our ancient ancestors—especially the Minoan sailors—had discovered this natural ability? It was certainly known in ancient times, but never recorded as far back as this. Imagine the Minoan sailors, coming home with a great cargo of goods for sale. Perhaps they just want to inform their family or shareholders of their return, and what better way than by pigeon! Long before the boat is visible there arrives a message, saying, 'Almost home—get the table laid'.

The owner that first sighted the great tea clippers in Victorian times stood a better chance of getting the best prices for his cargo, if he and only he was in the know. Perhaps these ancient mariners carried with them birds native to a range of different ports. In that way, you could inform any port of your imminent arrival and steal a march on the competition. So was the dove a Minoan ship to shore communication tool? I see nothing extraordinary in thinking this, especially as it involves sailors who were competent enough to sail the Great Green. Then from my research at the Ashmolean Museum in Oxford, I knew that the Minoans were well acquainted with doves or pigeons, their likeness celebrated in all kinds of artefacts. For example a pigeon with her brood, as a vase. Again as a vase, a painted pigeon standing on a fish motif. There was a signet ring showing a man holding not one, but two pigeons. If pigeons were this well known, then surely their homing instincts were appreciated too. Plus I can add to this theory that archaeologists have reconstructed a wall fresco discovered in Akrotiri, on the island of Thira. Here you can see quite clearly ships carrying passengers and heading swiftly for harbour. Also if you look very carefully you can discern, on the long curved prows of these ships, some strange structures. I consider that at least one of these is a bird cage. There also appear to be what look like perches. Is it my imagination, or do I really see a dove or pigeon situated on one? Perhaps it is just coincidence, and the artist has put the bird in that position to show it merely flying by. Yet somehow I don't think so. To me the bird is on the perch.

So, if one dove brought back a message, a green olive leaf, was this the same one that Noah let loose in the first place? Or was it, say, from an agent on a coastal shore well away from Crete? If the latter, could the message have been, 'Welcome home—we've been expecting you'? The answer to that is no. The underlying mechanics with homing pigeons are this: you leave one in a pair at home, and transport its mate as many miles away as you like—300 if necessary. You tie a small, light weight cylinder to its leg, into which is inserted the message. This wouldn't necessarily be written, but could be a symbol—perhaps a leaf, provided the recipient knew what that meant. The pigeon, upon its release, instantly picks up its bearings and flies these hundreds of miles at sixty to eighty miles per hour, straight for home and its mate.

Can a pigeon be trained to return to a mate that is subsequently placed on a ship that puts out to sea? No, it can't. Homing pigeons are precisely that—antennas for home. If you want to send a message to Port Z you have to take a pigeon with you originating in Port Z. So how did Noah or the ship's captain receive this message when he was at sea? There is only one answer. He was already in Port Z when a pigeon arrived from some other city. Although Noah's pigeon only carried a plucked olive leaf, we automatically think of this as a sign of peace. Yet could it be that in reality the captain was waiting in Port Z for a message from further inland? A message giving Noah, his people and livestock, permission to come ashore in peace—what really amounts to an early form of immigration authority and passport control.

The way I see it is this. The first pigeon was released as they approached Port Z. They then arrived at Port Z and received a message from City X. Obviously the bearer of this message would have been a pigeon originating in Port Z, then taken to City X, where it could be released. To send a message from Port Z to City X would require either the captain or the port authorities to release a pigeon whose mate was in City Z, but this would have been sufficient to announce that Noah and company were coming ashore.

Now if Noah and his people weren't transported via a shipping company to Canaan, we must ask whatever happened to the stock of fine timber forming the ark, but now available for recycling. This he had protected from the water by pitching it with tar, inside and out.

Pitching the joints of a ship makes it leak proof, but pitching inside and out protects it (in my opinion) from the sinister wood loving teredo worm, which lived in the warm waters of the Mediterranean. We hear that Noah landed and became a husbandman and grew grapes and made wine and got drunk in his tent. To grow grapes takes three years. To make wine, another year. That was a total of four years living in a tent. Now why live in a tent for that long when it was ample time to dismantle the boat and build a log cabin? It has been put to me that Mt Ararat is too high to grow grapes, therefore Noah would have to come down off the mountain to do so, leaving his ark behind. Yet the ark coming to rest on Mt Ararat can't be right. It's high, but not as high as Mt Everest. If God is going to cover the world in water, why leave out Tibet? Some scholars will say it was the ice caps melting, this being the end of an ice age, but that would mean that it took only seven months for the ice to melt. If, then, the water receded, we must logically conclude that the ice age came back with a vengeance, all in a few days!

It must be remembered that the early Hebrews had little history to base their religious ceremonies on. All through their wanderings into Mesopotamia, and then into Egypt, they appropriated bits and pieces

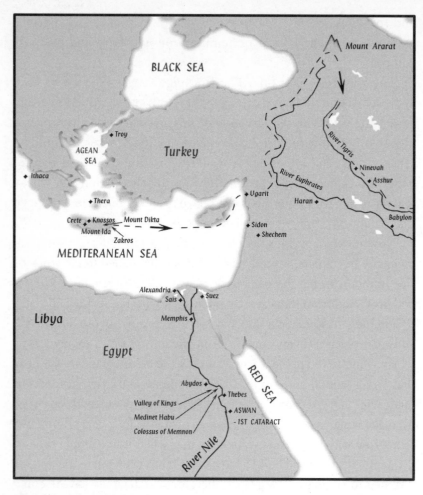

Noah's Route circa 1450 BC — — — — — —

from the cultures of other peoples. From the *Britannica Encyclopaedia* I quote the following extract: 'Though plain when compared with some of the learned literary creation of Mesopotamia, Canaan, Egypt, the earliest biblical writings are so imbued with contemporary ancient Middle Eastern elements that the once held assumption that Israelite religion began on a primitive level must be rejected.' So here we have confirmation that the Hebrews were quite happy to absorb parts of other religions in order to enhance their own, just as they absorbed other peoples' places, even though that might only be by naming

Noah's grandchildren after them. They must also have absorbed the language of Mesopotamia. The point to be made here is how much of their religion was theirs, and not merely adopted?

Personally I consider most of Genesis and Exodus to be true to general events, with minor alterations to suit their creed. Yet they remained true to a one god deity, when all around them were religions sporting whole families of supernatural beings. Why didn't they just give in to the fashions and allow themselves to be assimilated into these other belief systems? Surely that would have been the most sensible thing to do. The fact is they didn't because they had seen the power of their God when Thira or Santorini blew itself sky high. I say Thira and Santorini, which might sound confusing, for in reality there was once one island called Kalliste, meaning 'the most beautiful'. It was the volcano on this island that blasted it in two, forming the present day Thira and Santorini. So whatever local god was on offer, they weren't going to accept him at the risk of upsetting the God they knew.

Every scholar of ancient Mesopotamia believes that the story of Gilgamesh and his flood was *the* flood of the Hebrews. Yet what if there was a Mesopotamian river flood? A flood where Utnapishtim, who doesn't have one god but many, saves himself by building an ark. A very similar story indeed, its even having a dove and a raven. I considered this carefully, and according to David Rohl, in his book *Legend, the Genesis of Civilisation* (pp153 154), in 1872 the Akkadian linguist George Smith began to translate part of a tablet from the seventh century archives of King Ashurbanipal of Assyria. This was the Gilgamesh epic. If we take the legend of Utnapishtim's Babylonian flood as the equivalent of Noah's (some books refer to him as Ziusudra), we can see that the stories are very similar. Utnapishtim (Ziusudra) was overtaken by a cosmic disaster caused by one of his gods, Enlil, who was angered by the tumult made by mankind. Another god Ea warned Utnapishtim that Enlil was going to flood the earth and destroy man. Forewarned, Utnapishtim escapes by building a boat, taking his family and animals on board. As the flood recedes his boat comes to rest on a mountain. After his deliverance, to show his gratitude, he sacrifices to all the other gods except Enlil, the one that caused the flood. Enlil gets angry at this, but the other gods intercede, to the effect that Utnapishtim was in the right. Enlil accepts this and makes Utnapishtim immortal, sending him to live in the garden of Dilmun.

Again, something doesn't fit. It's that raven again. Sailors on the Euphrates and Tigris rivers would have had no need to use a raven as a direction indicator, simply because they could always see the river banks and the direction of the current. It's possible a carrier pigeon may have been useful, but not to the same extent as at sea, the distances not being so great. As for the date or time, I consider my Hebrews to be in Mesopotamia in 1350BC, well before 800. I see no reason why they couldn't be telling their story of the flood to the peoples of these rivers, and there is no reason why the Mesopotamian peoples didn't incorporate it into their Gilgamesh story. It's this seemingly insignificant detail with the raven and the dove which gives it away, and convinces me that the Gilgamesh story comes later. It may even be that the Gilgamesh story never existed, but was taken wholesale from the Hebrews and mixed up with their own gods. After all, before the introduction of television, story telling would have been a way of earning a pound or two, to such an extent that one like this could easily pass into Sumerian folklore. I could be wrong, but neither the raven nor the dove fits with the everyday navigation of river craft, yet certainly both can be associated with sea going vessels. And again, there are only two places in the Mediterranean where a raven would be used—sailing west to Malta, and east to Cyprus and then on to Palestine.

Although the stories are similar, I think you'll agree they're not *that* similar. With Gilgamesh, there is a god who is one of many. Furthermore he is not inclined to help Utnapishtim, and is angry at the tumult made by man. Tumult is a commotion of a multitude. Instantly I am reminded of the noise on a large construction project.

In the Bible it is quite clear that the Hebrews were working in construction on Asshur, Babylon, Nineveh and Nimrud. They had become sub contract brickmakers, and even took their trade into Egypt. There is some indication of this noise in Genesis 11: 6 9. Even the place of Babel means scene of confusion or noisy assembly. This isn't a god getting angry, it's an old high priest getting upset about the noise problem and sleepless nights. In Utnapishtim's flood there is only one disaster with no mention of a previous one, such as the Adam and Eve expulsion. Nor was Noah made immortal or sent to live in a garden. Nevertheless he did make a vineyard and got drunk. I think therefore there was only one flood, and that was his. Notwithstanding that, it is the raven and the doves that are so important. They are original, and so unexpected, and if to Noah they're worth a mention, then it tells us that Noah was out at sea.

There is another flood, nearer to Thira, the flood of Zeus, or Deucalion flood. So reads *Colliers Encyclopaedia*: 'When Zeus, the king of the Gods, resolved to destroy humanity by a flood, Deucalion constructed an ark in which, according to one version, he and his wife rode it out and landed on Mt Parnassus, in southern Greece.' To me this looks like a westward escape from Thira, while Noah's is an eastward one to Canaan. In both cases they differ from the Utnapishtim legend, because there is only one God. As I have said, Thira's awesome eruption must have been a legend maker—the aggression of Jupiter and Saturn, the new gods versus the old, a veritable clash of Titans.

The beauty of friends—on to whom of course I have bounced these ideas—is that they all want to play the devil's advocate. It has been asked of me, why couldn't Noah be riding the high seas of the Persian Gulf? That is a good question, since this would put Noah in the region of the Tigris and Euphrates rivers. Again, it's the black raven that comes to my rescue. If we look at an atlas of the Persian Gulf, or of the Red Sea, we see these stretches of water running virtually north to south. Neither is wide—about 170 miles for the Red Sea, and 140 for the Persian Gulf. So, in these instances, if you went north or south you hugged the coastline. Going east or west was just a matter of following the rising or sinking sun, with the result that you just couldn't miss coming to land. If our sailors were travelling at four knots, they would make landfall in thirty five to forty five hours—or two days. Even if they left shore with little or no food or water, they still had every reasonable chance of making the other side.

In both of these waterways there are few if any islands to break up the journey, so there would have been absolutely no reason to have a raven on board. Whereas the Mediterranean is wider and longer by far.

If a sailor headed east or west from Crete, he would need his raven in order to find Malta and Cyprus. Heading south the raven would not have been necessary, since Africa would eventually rear itself up. Heading north from Crete there is a cluster of islands, the Cyclades, most of which become visible as the other land is left behind. So, as you can see, this simple mention of a raven, released to fly to and fro until the waters abated, can only be all bound up in a system for plotting direction. Of course, I could be wrong—but I'd like to meet the professor who will put his reputation on the line, by advancing a counter argument.

We mustn't forget too that there are more impressive birds that could have been mentioned by Noah. He could have said an eagle, a symbol destined to figure in the life of many nations as one of strength. It can fly high, it can't swim, and it loves land. Yet to catch an eagle is a different matter from catching a raven. A raven or crow makes economic sense, since both are scavengers and are easily trapped.

As for the ark resting on the mountains of Ararat, this is just not logically possible. I can only comment that perhaps this was the high watermark for Noah and his people's journey, as they continued to search for land they could call their own. Mt Ararat is only 120 miles north of Nineveh, and perhaps it was from there that they decided to return. More on that later. For the moment, it is my humble opinion that the vessel had deposited Noah and left for another voyage. Here again, I don't think it was Noah and his family—I consider it was all those who followed him and his one true God, a God who had made man in his own image.

So who were these seafarers? If Noah was a farmer migrating from Crete, then the people living in Crete were the Minoans—a name given to a lost civilisation which was only rediscovered in about 1900 by Sir Arthur Evans. They were great traders and seafarers of the Mediterranean up to 1450BC. What happened in 1450BC to make them cease not only this trade but as a civilisation? Seismologists have confirmed that the greatest natural disaster took place on the island of Thira just eighty kilometres north of Crete. The island blew up and some seventy cubic kilometres blew up and away, to be deposited as ash on the middle and eastern part of Crete. This was so thick as to cover the pastures of the mountainsides and completely choke the streams. Scientists estimate that 120 hydrogen bombs would have been needed to wreak comparable damage.

Did Noah relate this event when rain and ash poured out of the sky on to the land, more importantly on to *his* land? Rain that was going to cover the world in water and kill off all those other populations who were so upsetting God. Well, yes, he did relate it, for it rained for forty days and forty nights—a numerical exaggeration not so much applied to a length of time, but to do with the sheer volume of water. Noah, when he arrived with his followers at the sea shore, had never before seen so much, since they were all simple God fearing farmers who belonged to mountain pastures, whose streams or small lakes were a trickle in comparison. Moreover the God they feared was He who abided with them, and seemed—if we take the story of Cain and Abel to favour shepherds and pastoral folk generally—a God who had made man in His own image. That, according to legend, was exactly the character of the young Zeus, who was similarly associated with the mountains of Crete, and who, if he had not made man in his own image, was at least in the image of man.

There isn't much of a tide in the Mediterranean, although it does exist. It *would* have been evident to Noah and his band of devotees—devotees to a brand new religion—waiting to go on board ship with their livestock. They would have seen the waters rising. Once at sea and heading away from Crete, Noah would definitely have seen, as he looked behind him, his island slowly slip beneath the waters until it had sunk completely. As his Cretan hills disappeared, he would have looked about him to see nothing other than the sea and the sky. To him and his followers it would have been self evident, even if it wasn't raining where they were, that it must be pouring torrents somewhere else. How else could the waters rise up? This is why I am apt to say that it wouldn't have to rain for forty days and forty nights to convince farmer Noah that what he saw was a deluge.

There are other connections between Noah and the Minoans. Enos, an uncle of his, had a good Minoan name. Orthodox Jews to this day still wear a peculiar hairstyle with long striking side locks, much as those portrayed as Minoan in the wall paintings at Knossos. Here the picture of the priest king is seen to be winding a band around his forearm. Was this a forerunner of the Jewish phylactery? There are too Minoan kernos, archaeologically a mystery, forerunners it seems of the Jewish seven stemmed candelabrum. To cap it we have, in Ezekiel, 28: 13 14, Ezekiel himself cursing the king of Tyre: 'Thou hast been in Eden the garden of God; every precious stone was thy covering…thou wast upon the holy mountain of God; thou hast walked up and down in the midst of the stones of fire.' It is clear from this that Ezekiel believed the ancestors of Tyre had once lived in Eden and dwelt upon the mountain of God before their fall from grace. This is a view evidently shared by David Rohl, whose *Legends* sets out the same theory.

Did Ezekiel have the answer to the puzzle—for Tyre was a Phoenician city—and the Phoenicians were descendants of the Minoans? When the Minoans fled Crete after Santorini's eruption, they made landfall all around the shores of the Mediterranean. Some took up industry. Others continued their seafaring way of life, as pirates. Some became legitimate sea traders, and it was these latter who became known as the Phoenicians. If they came from Crete, and they walked upon the mountain among the stones of fire, then their ancestors where walking on the island of Santorini before it exploded.

There are also records from Pharaoh Amenophis II's time—1436 1413BC—showing that there was unrest in Canaan due to the arrival of marauding bands of Apiru, or Hapiru—a new people who seem to have come from nowhere. For a long time scholars have identified these people with the Hebrews of the Old Testament, but most Egyptian philologists (specialists in ancient languages) agree with Sir Alan Gardiner that it is simply a term meaning 'bandit' or 'outcast', and therefore not necessarily connected with the Hebrews at all. From this we can say that someone has made a connection between the words 'Hebrew', 'Hapiru', 'bandit' and 'outcast'. Let's for a moment forget the Hebrews, and let's also put Thira's eruption at 1450BC. People start to migrate, and whoever they are they are homeless, unable to acquire land of their own. They are forced to wander, seeking out some promise of a land, being not quite strong enough for an all out fight. One could liken them to gypsies. And as with gypsies, it needn't be them who steal your goods, but a 'good' neighbour, who conveniently puts the blame on to these nomads, whose words of protestation wouldn't be believed. Consequently their name is blackened even more. Therefore if Hapiru really means 'bandit' and 'outcast', that still doesn't discount these people as nomads. We don't trust gypsies so we make them outcasts. And isn't a bandit too an outcast?

Nevertheless these Hapiru seem just the people to have migrated from Crete. We don't know what happened to them after they created unrest in Canaan, except that they were moved on. They couldn't go westwards out to sea, or south into powerful Egypt. This leaves north into present day Turkey, although much more inviting would be east into the lush river valleys of the Euphrates and Tigris. For a time the Hapiru seem to have left the Canaanites in peace, then about a hundred years later they once more descended into Canaan. Dare I say, but it seems to be exactly the time that Abraham arrived!

Are there any other connections between the Jews and the Greeks that may have some bearing on Noah fleeing from Crete? There is. It is the legend of Hercules and his seventh labour, which was to capture the Cretan bull. This he did single handed and took the monster back to Mycenae. Eurystheus dedicated the bull to Hera (who was the wife of the ever unfaithful Zeus), but the goddess set the bull free as she loathed a gift that redounded to Hercules' glory, and so drove it to Sparta. Now here's the punch line. In Josephus' book *The Antiquities of the Jews*, he tells us that in 143BC the Jews sent an embassy to the Spartans, with whom they claimed kinship. Kinship means blood ties— so what possible right had the Jews to even consider kinship with Sparta? Where in heaven's name did they come up with that idea? Jews are supposed to come from the Euphrates and Tigris river country, miles away to the east, with not sufficient ties in Greece to have established kinship. Or is that correct?

According to the book *Religions* by Alan Brown, John Rankin and Angela Wood, 'The Jewish people were never actually born...they became distinctive because of their experience of a unique God, just, merciful, who gives human beings laws and values so that they too can be merciful. A God who can be felt in the pattern of human history.'—just so with Zeus too. To say that the Jewish race wasn't actually born, is simply to say that no one has a clue as to where they originated.

There have been many theories put forward as to Noah's flood. Mine isn't the first and it won't be the last. Only recently on television there was a programme explaining that what we now know as the Black Sea was once dry land, and that it was somewhere in this basin that Noah and his people lived. Then at some point the Mediterranean burst through the Bosporus and poured into this basin. That prompted Noah to build his ark, while the flood rose up, filling the Black Sea, and subsequently leaving his ark at rest on Mt Ararat. In its favour, Mt Ararat isn't that far from the Black Sea—some 250 miles. But this is a theory with serious flaws. Firstly the water must have risen not only enough to fill the Black Sea, but a further 16 17,000 feet higher, to reach Mt Ararat. Secondly the Bosporus is not opening but closing. If you look on your map you will see the huge range of mountains that are Turkey, of which Mt Ararat is one. These aren't there for fun. The whole landmass is rising and is being pushed towards Greece. I strongly suspect this is caused by India still pushing into Asia and in turn still pushing Tibet higher. Thirdly the Black Sea produces more water from its great river than it wants. Therefore if any sea is going to burst forth, it will be the Black Sea foaming into the Mediterranean. The current running through this gap is quite strong, as is suggested by Jason and his Argonauts. They needed a fifty oared craft to overcome it. Just to underline that point, the Royal Navy in World War I had great difficulty in sending submarines from the Mediterranean through this narrow Sea of Marmora, due to that same strong current coming out. Fourthly if the Mediterranean had gushed into a dry Black Sea basin, the area being so big would have meant

Palace of Knossos: fresco of the young prince,
sometimes called the Priest King.

months for the waters to rise. Therefore the bigger the area covered, the slower the rise. So, that would have been a flood you could have happily walked away from.

At least *my* flood is unique—not because it has more reasoning, and a more convincing historical context, but because logic dictates there wasn't one. But what of Mt Ararat? This high mountain I am not dismissing from these events. I am a strong believer that the Old Testament holds a lot of truths. To get Mt Ararat back in the story, what about if Noah landed in Canaan, but was told to move on, just like our present day Boat People? And how appropriate for Noah's first grandson to be named Canaan. They moved east and within 120 miles found the River Euphrates. They turned north, following it for ease of passage—the water, the green pasture. In this way they would come to within fifty miles of Mt Ararat, where the land is cold and bleak. This was their high watermark, and now it was time to head back south, when they eventually came to Babylon. Either way, as the Tigris also rises in this area, they could just as easily have come down that river to Nineveh and then over the plains of Shinar from the east to Babylon, just as the Bible states. Of course, from there the Hebrews started to move from legend into history. This was under Abraham, as they headed back to the Promised Land—a land they were already familiar with.

According to the Jewish rabbi Josephus, the exodus took place in 1447BC. Scholars are suspicious about this, since it doesn't conform to historical events in Egypt. It would be convenient to think that somewhere in the songs and stories passed down, somebody got it wrong, and that 1447BC relates to Noah's exodus from Crete. In that case it would fit nicely with the seismological dating of Thira's second and most powerful eruption, that of 1450.

So, gentle reader, in my humble opinion the case for the defence on Tacitus' claim that the Jews originated in Crete does bear scrutiny. However, there is a sting in the tale. Some 1,600 years ago we banished those Olympian gods to the outer limits of our solar system. If you look up on a clear night, there you will see Mercury, Saturn, bright Venus, red Mars and the giant Jupiter, who still protects planet Earth. Its enormous gravitational pull attracts all the space debris heading on a collision course for us, and the other planets. Now, if you listen very carefully, on the night breeze you just might hear the gods laughing. For it seems that if Noah did flee from the flood of his God, then he also fled the flood of Zeus. And if Noah is indeed Minoan, then his god *is* Zeus. So, it would appear that one of the gods—the father of the gods himself—never ever did leave, and has been here all the time. Ah ha, I hear you say—but Zeus was the father of *all* the gods. This is true indeed, except that there must have been a time at the outset of that religion when there was only him alone. Later, he (or man's imaginary forces) created the other gods. So here then is a good case for Jove being in reality Jehovah—but then that's another story...

Israeli Espionage, Two and a Half Thousand Years Ago

I have stumbled on an incredible piece of luck, which I cannot rush you through, but will take it step by step, and leave you to draw your own conclusions. I believe though that you, like me, once you have read this, and put the various twos and twos together, will arrive at a very emphatic four.

Espionage is an old and dangerous craft. History has recorded cases older than 2,500 years—but to have found a further example to add to that tally is more than interesting. Most countries steal the secrets and designs of others, if not for self protection then to be one up on their neighbours. In general they are military secrets, but in the case I am going to present, you will see it as unique—a military secret innocently stolen for the greater glory of God. I had read the description of the ark time and time again, and I had even discovered how long was a cubit. When the ark's cubits were converted to feet or metres, it turned out to be big indeed for its time in history. Nevertheless, whatever size you called a cubit, if you drew it out in the proportions laid down in the Bible, the vessel was long and narrow. That is, it wasn't some fat waddling merchant ship for carrying cargo. It was a greyhound of the sea, and greyhounds were hunters. Indeed this vessel could only be a war ship. This was my first clue, but there in Genesis—6: 14 16— was another:

Make thee an ark of gopher wood;
Rooms shalt thou make in the ark,
And shalt pitch it within and without with pitch.

And this is the fashion which thou shalt make it of:
The length of the ark shall be three hundred cubits,
The breadth of it fifty cubits, and the height of it thirty cubits.

A window shalt thou make to the ark,
And in a cubit shalt thou finish it above;
And the door of the ark shalt thou set in the side thereof;
With lower, second, and third stories shalt thou make it.

It was the lower, second, and third stories that gave it away. Treated in and out with pitch indicated it was possibly more of a sea than a river vessel, and the three decks and that emphasis on speed suggest that what is being narrated is the design and dimensions of a Greek trireme—the warship that allowed the Greeks to conquer the Mediterranean in the sixth century BC. So what is this ship doing in the Bible when the period of history we are reading about would be long before Abraham came out of Mesopotamia—or Joseph went into Egypt—or Moses came out (about 1200BC)? The early parts of the Talmud or the Old Testament can be dated to about 700BC, and I suggest to my readers that it is at this moment that a Jewish scholar is for the first time recording this period of his history. Whoever this was, he was mathematical with it, having just completed a number of arithmetic sums for his pupils to copy out (Genesis 5: 3 32—who begat whom, and the years they spanned). Herein may be the generations of Adam, but if you look closely it's all simply a lesson in adding up. Let's take a look at verses 9 11:

And Enos lived ninety years, and begat Cainan:
And Enos lived after he begat Cainan eight hundred and fifteen
    years,
And begat sons and daughters:

And all the days of Enos were nine hundred and five years:
And he died.

One could translate this as follows—

$$90 + 815 = 905$$

—but of course I doubt if they had a plus or an equals sign, so it had to be learned in some other way. What better way than a story! For didn't we of a certain generation in primary school learn our sums when our teacher said, *A farmer has ten cows, five sheep and two goats: how many animals does he have?*

What is interesting about these biblical examples I refer to is that there are twenty five numbers used. Some are in the hundreds, some in the tens, and some are units. If we analyse these closely we find that nine numbers end with zero, seven end with a five, three end with a seven, five end with a two, and one ends with a nine. If this is an arithmetic primer, then it would indicate that five and zero are popular, possibly showing that fingers on both hands were of importance to any calculation.

However, I digress—for all I am trying to bring to your attention is that the author was mathematically minded. He was writing about the ark of Noah, and living—if I may hazard a calculated guess—at about 600BC, possibly in the city of Haifa, with a good view of the harbour. He was probably scratching his head and wondering if he could exercise a bit of poetic licence, such as I exercise myself, filling out the story of Noah and his ark.

As he sat there thinking, around the headland came the biggest ship he had ever seen or was ever likely to see. With 150 white tipped oars flashing in the sunlight, dipping up and down in unison, this graceful vessel, this warship shot across the bright azure and tied up within the harbour walls. Whether he girded up his loins and rushed down there, or gently strolled to the water's edge, we shall never know—though he must have been excited. For this was the very boat which he wanted as Noah's ark.

It so happened that the Greek trireme was the secret weapon of its day, which although plainly there for all to see, would have been very conscientiously guarded. I imagine our mathematical scholar made some inquiries as to the vessel's size, and was told to go away. He would have seen the three decks, and might have seen too that the oars had been shipped onboard on arrival. Or possibly he didn't notice this—for likewise there was something else he didn't spot—which leads me to believe he was so intent on learning the boat's dimensions that he decided to do an espionage job, and measure it by night. Bear with me as I make this deduction—you *will* see what I mean.

With modern tourism, many of us have had the opportunity to visit the Mediterranean. The water is clear—you can see to the sea bed some forty feet or so below. If our Israeli scholar had visited the vessel by day, he too would have peered into the deep blue clear waters, and so would have observed the sting that went with its prow—namely the great bronze beak that was fixed to and protruding from it just below the surface of the sea. It was this weapon that made the Greek trireme supreme. Rowed by 150 highly trained and very fit oarsmen, it could be propelled at great speed, like a torpedo into the side of an enemy ship. The oars would be reversed on the instant of initial impact—the shock of the collision—and the great beak pulled free to allow water to pour into the hold of the target. In fact it ripped a hole that was almost impossible to repair before the ship went under. It was to this end that it was critical that the beak should be below the water line, since a ship holed above the waves wouldn't be mortally damaged.

How can I presume all this? Well, once I'd discovered the possibility that the author was modelling his Noah's ark on the trireme, I scoured the archives in search of dimensions for the latter. It appeared that Napoleon III had built one in 1860, but it was impractical and couldn't be rowed and ended up as a display. Mussolini had had one built, but with the same results. Despite this, and although there were lots of accounts, and even archaeological remains of the sheds that had once housed these swans of the sea, nobody knew their size. This meant that whoever could find these dimensions would have the weight of proof in his favour, if it could be shown that the 150 requisite rowers could easily and successfully propel it.

In researching this I tried to find as accurately as possible the imperial equivalent of a cubit. My dictionary gave it as about eighteen inches, although in those ancient days it was very much your own personal measure, being the distance from the tip of your middle finger to the end of your elbow. Lanky lads would arrive at a different measurement from others who were short and squat. Nevertheless, supposing my dictionary definition to be a workable definition, then 300 cubits, being the recorded length of the ark, would put her length in line with that of HMS *Hermes*, a modern day warship. Interestingly, when considering *Hermes'* length to width ratio, she turns out not to be as sleek as the ark would have been. I think therefore that the ark of the Bible was trying to masquerade as a plump old lady or merchant ship, with a cargo of breeding stock.

As luck would have it, when I was staying with nautical friends of mine—Terry and Liz Hall at Birdham—I mentioned this problem. Their daughters Alex and Louise shot off to bring me a book on ancient dimensions, from which I derived the following:

1 cubit = 480 mm or 18.898 inches

—therefore the breadth of the ark at 50 cubits was 78.74 ft, and its length of 300 cubits 472.45 ft. All I had got to do now was find myself a trireme.

A first clue which told me I was on the right trail came from Peter Connolly's book *Greece and Rome at War*, which offered information on an early trireme (fifth century BC). I noted the measures and was reassured to find its length was six times its width—as was the case with Noah's ark. My breakthrough came when I discovered that in 1987 three English designers, Frank Walsh, John Morrison and John Coates, after sifting through every scrap of ancient literature, plus archaeological evidence that included ancient Greek pots—and with financial help from the Greek government—built a full scale model. When 150 oarsmen came together from every rowing club in Britain, and arrived in Piraeus, the world was to see for the first time in some 2,000 years a Greek trireme beat gracefully out to sea.

When I first saw this on television I could not help but be impressed. With power and majesty the 150 white tipped oars flashed together as one, breaking the surface of the sea into a white spume. With each beat the ship surged forward, cutting through the water with dread intent. There on the prow were the painted eyes, just as in the days of Jason, on his ship *Argo*, manned by his Argonauts. If you looked carefully, you could just discern the plume of water feet ahead of the bows. For here cutting through the waves was that lethal sting, the great bronze ram. As I have already said, the whole purpose to the craft was to point it into the side of an enemy vessel. Then, with every muscle straining, an increased beat of the oars would send it surging forward on its destructive mission. Indeed the ship's very shape was designed for this and nothing else.

It would have been difficult to urinate and fart in comfort on this vessel—or so wrote an ancient Greek playwright (it was comments like these that assisted the three English designers in their task). If it was that cramped, how was one to live on it in company with nervous animals? I think you weren't, and I think it was to the honour of the gods that *Olympia* was launched. Her length was 121.5 ft, and her width 19.7 ft—a ratio a touch more than the 1 to 6 I was looking for. I wasn't too perturbed, and began to look for any relationships between the ark and the trireme. The width of the trireme was 19.7 ft, while the width of the ark was 78.74 ft. The ark was therefore 3.997 times wider than the trireme, or near as damn it 4 times wider. However, the length of the trireme was 121.5 ft, and the length of the ark was 472.45 ft—which made the ark only 3.888 times longer. This had me worried. The figures weren't consistent. What had gone wrong?

I was about to close the book on this latest theory of mine, when it struck me that I had measured the *Olympia* out of water, with the great bronze beak exposed, and had done so from the plans. But what if my Jewish rabbi had measured up *his* trireme and not seen the bronze beak under the water? I measured up the *Olympia* again, leaving off her protruding beak, which under normal operating conditions would in any case have been below the surface of the water. This now gave me a new and shorter length of 118.42 ft. Comparing this with the ark's gave me a quotient of 3.9897—and if that isn't 4 times bigger, I'll eat my hat!

How could you miss this ram below the clear blue waters of the sea, which was then far less polluted than it is now? The answer can only be that when he asked permission to inspect the trireme he was told by the Greek guards to push off. Not to be deterred, our Jewish writer, reporter and scholar had gone back in the dead of night, possibly rowed around the vessel and measured it up in the dark. If triremes weren't meant for luxury living, then almost certainly the whole crew would have gone ashore for the night. As for the guard, perhaps he wasn't too worried as he watched our inquisitive scribe paddle around the ship—for after all, he wouldn't have gone aboard. This same scribe though was a good reporter, and good reporters always want the full facts. That it was night, and he missed this extra but centrally important part of the Greek warship, was hardly his fault.

Now that he had his figures—75 cubits long, 12.5 feet wide—he rushed back to his tenement and papyrus. Like all good story tellers he probably began to think of the boat as twice its real size, and by the time he got to his pen and ink that factor had already swollen to four. This was to the glory of God, by the use, possibly, of a magical or sacred mathematical formula—the figure 2 (and its multiplication by 2) being something special in Israeli religious thinking. That aside, in my mind he has gone down in my history of the world as one of Israel's first agents of espionage.

I must at this stage apologise to my readers, for with the zeal and energy I have devoted to this puzzle, I have forgotten to draw similar comparisons to a merchant ship of 600BC. A typical example would be 98 ft by 23 ft, shorter and fatter than the trireme—and this I would have expected. Comparison with the ark shows the latter to be 4.82 times longer, but only 3.42 times wider. (As you can see, there is no comparison.) We can conclude then that the all important dimensions *were* taken from a Greek trireme, measured and recorded in scripture some time after the sixth century BC (before this the trireme hadn't been invented).

Now it's true that my imagination has worked overtime, to create a picture of our rabbi obtaining his dimensions, but what this doesn't tell us is the dimensions of Noah's ark, or where and when it was launched, or where it came to rest—for whatever ship this was, it wasn't Noah's ark.

For those whose minds will run to this, my height is 5' 11". I have measured from my finger tip to my elbow, and this distance—my cubit—is 18.1 inches. Working with that as a ratio, a person with a cubit measure of 18.898 inches would have been about 6' 2" tall. Was this the height of our Israeli spy? Tall he might have been, but whoever he was, he didn't know a merchant ship from a battleship, although he did recognise a big craft when he saw one, God bless him!

That Old Hot Chestnut, Atlantis

*A*tlantis—everybody seems to have written about this fabled land. Now that I do too, I find I am doing so almost as an apology.

It was while researching the great eruption of Thira or Santorini, in 1450BC, that it occurred to me that here was a classic example of a natural phenomenon spawning a legend. It had been ten times greater than the recent eruption of Mt Helen—and not only that…it was in the right geographical location to have caused the Atlantian catastrophe. The island on which the volcano sat was once called Kalliste, the 'most beautiful', but having blown itself apart now forms two islands—Thira and Santorini—just eighty kilometres north of Crete. Crete—the island of the mysterious Minoans, who seem to have vanished from their island home in a night and a day.

Now, wouldn't logic and common sense dictate that if the eruption of Thira had been so great, then other countries in immediate proximity would have heard about it?

What intrigues me particularly is where scholars have theorised Atlantis might be found. Most of these theories I find not at all convincing. Yet it's an interesting legend, and as such is a repository of considerable information—so much so that there ought to be *something* in it. You might ask, so many scholars having explored this, and come up with a variety of places, what right I have I got to poke my nose in? The answer is this. In researching my various writing projects, some striking parallels have appeared, between the Atlantian story, the Minoans and the Bible.

For two to run together is a coincidence, but when all three start showing similarities, one has got to take notice.

Our first indication is that Egypt had recorded a terrible Minoan catastrophe. Crete is so near to Egypt that there is absolutely no doubt that the Minoans were trading there before the eruption of Thira. But because the legend is of Atlantis, one popular belief has been of a lost world somewhere in the Atlantic—or even further afield. Yet how did this legend begin, and why should I consider it was Egypt's answer to the factual eruption on Thira?

In former times it was as popular to go on holiday as it is today. During the seventeenth to the nineteenth centuries the nobility and the wealthy upper reaches of society took what was called the Grand Tour—a tour of Europe whose purpose was to broaden one's knowledge. Solon, an Athenian of c590BC, also took time out. He went to a place called Sais, which is at one of the junctions of the Nile in the delta area. He went there asking questions as to what Egypt knew concerning the early history of Greece. A priest said to him, 'Solon, you Hellenes [Greeks] are never anything but children, and there is not an old man among you.' When asked what he meant, the priest replied, 'You all have young minds. You never inquire into your past, nor into any science which is hoary with age. There is a story, which even you have preserved, that one day Phaethon, son of Helios [better known as Apollo, who daily drove the sun across the heaven], having yoked the steeds in his father's chariot, because he was not able to drive them in his father's path, burnt up all that was on the earth. Zeus had to come to the rescue, though Phaethon was destroyed by a thunderbolt.' Though when on the other hand the gods purged the earth with a deluge of water, the survivors were herdsmen and shepherds who dwelt in the mountains. Those who like Solon lived in cities were carried by the rivers into the sea.

Where did this legend begin? One could say it was with the records of Egypt, first brought to light by that Egyptian priest. It was then given to Solon, who in turn took it back to Greece and passed it on to Dropides, who told it to Critias the Senior, an old man of nearly ninety, who in his turn told it to another Critias, who was Plato's cousin. Critias died in 403BC when Plato was twenty four, and Critias informed Plato he had heard it from Critias the Elder, when he was a youth. Up to then the story had been passed on orally. Now Plato (427 347BC) put it down on paper or papyrus and recorded it in *The Dialogues* (c390BC). By then it was already 200 years on from Solon's time, and Plato conceded he had had to think hard to remember how it went. It was on his way home (so said Plato to Socrates) that he communicated the tale to his companions, in so far as he remembered it. After he had left them he recovered nearly all of it—this was during the night—by thinking very hard.

Truly, as is often said, the lessons of our childhood make a wonderful impression on our memories. Like all tales, one is tempted to add to it, yet there *is* an original story here, it's being so difficult to create a lie entire. The basic embryo of any tale enfolds the germ of its truth. Professor B Jowett (Oxford), in his translation of Plato, goes so far as to say that no one knew better than he (than Plato) how to invent a noble lie. But he forgets that when Plato said that during the night he recovered nearly all of it, he referred to the lessons of his childhood. He was telling his audience things they already knew, but which we don't. The story had been given to Plato orally. He had learnt it by rote. Now as an adult he was having to recite it again and again, stanza by stanza, in order to get the whole thing out.

I am reminded of my uncle Harry, who at eighty two has difficulty in remembering who *he* his, let alone who I am. Yet he can, without pause or hesitation, recite word for word fifty seven verses of Lord Macaulay's *The Keeping of the Bridge*. All one has to do to get him going is, as a computer specialist might put it, cite the password and you're in. If I utter the first two lines—'Lars Porsena of Clusium / By the Nine Gods he swore'—my ancient relation sets off. He will even finish his recital by telling you that (and he has done this so many times it seems almost part of the poem) he learnt it when he was twelve and won a prize for his efforts. Many eastern people learn in this way. They do so by nodding their heads up and down to a rhythm. I wonder is this how Plato was taught? If so, then somehow it adds substance to his story as one that he had to remember, and suggests that he didn't make it up.

Professor Jowett concludes that the whole thing is a fiction dreamed up by Plato, for the purpose of boosting Greek morale in the face of Persia's growing might. Likewise M Martin in his analysis goes on to say that the tale rests on the authority of the Egyptian priest, who took pleasure in deceiving the Greeks. He (Plato) never appears to suspect that there is a greater deceiver or magician than this Egyptian priest—that is to say, Plato himself! This is a strange scholarly appraisal, for it doesn't matter whether Plato lies or not—if we accept that the Egyptian priest did tell Solon the story, then it is outside Plato's hands and is worth pursuing.

What is interesting is that when Professor Jowett wrote his analysis, in 1871, few people realised that Thira had been an active volcano. He certainly hadn't heard of the Minoans—it would be another twenty five years before their discovery by Sir Arthur Evans. In saying this I suggest it is even possible that Evans and Jowett were not the best of friends. According to Leonard Cottrell, Evans, at the age of thirty three, became keeper of the Ashmolean Museum, in Oxford. This was in 1884. The museum, founded in the seventeenth century by Elias Ashmole, had been so neglected, abused and mutilated by later generations that it had almost ceased to have any practical value. In fact its condition accurately reflected the indifference with which archaeology was regarded by Vice Chancellor Jowett (the very same) and other high ranking individuals of the university. But to Evans this was a challenge, which of course could have encompassed a test to Jowett's authority and beliefs. Then again, in Jowett's defence, why should he *not* have pooh poohed the legend? Plato puts Atlantis in the Atlantic, and in the Atlantic it had never been. And Sir Arthur Evans, in finally discovering the Minoans, wasn't going to lose his reputation to a will o' the wisp legend, which anyway had been put to bed in fairyland several times already.

Personally I can see a number of things in Plato's tale that may possibly be additions by him, but out of context. He mentions two springs—one hot water, one cold. This is similar to Homer's description of Troy. Another is Plato's description of the Atlantian harbour. The design is a channel from the sea that heads directly to a central island in a circular harbour. However, as you sail up this channel, there are other, concentric channels running around the inner circle. The whole design appears to be a small circle as the nucleus (a wharf), and radiating from that ever larger, alternating circles of land and water. A channel from the sea running straight through to the centre would enable you to moor your ship in whichever circular harbour you wished. The cost and manpower to build all this would be high if not crippling, and I suspect that Plato has exaggerated in order to get the point across that the harbour could accommodate a large number of vessels. Greece at this time depended for her own safety on her navy, and it wasn't difficult to understand that a large harbour meant also a large fleet—which was good for morale.

Is there an ancient harbour of this design? There is, and I have seen it. It is the harbour of Carthage. It is now of course an ancient ruin, and although big is difficult to see, so many houses having been built around it. However, as you fly back from Tunis to England, you pass directly over it, and can thereby get a very good idea of what it was like in its prime (if nothing to the size of Plato's Atlantian version!). I am not positive about this, but from my own research I would date it at about 400BC. If that is so, would it be possible that Plato had heard of it, and in taking note of its design embellished it in order to impress his audience? There would be reason for this, since the Greeks and the Carthaginians where plying for trade around the Mediterranean.

With the Carthaginian harbour, you can see a channel from the sea to an oblong wharf, which was for merchant ships. At the opposite end there is another channel which leads to a circular harbour, complete with a central island—and this is where war ships were moored. Missing are the other circular channels which would have encircled that. As for Carthage as Atlantis, it must be remembered that it wasn't colonised by the Phoenicians until after their escape from Tyre, which was long after Thira's eruption. The Phoenicians were a seafaring people who had settled originally in Palestine, and may even have been descendants of the sea going Minoans and refugees from Crete. Interestingly their language was a form of Semitic, and Semites are supposedly descended from Shem. The Phoenicians who colonised Carthage were from Tyre in Lebanon, forced out by internal political struggles. Legend has it that in c814BC Princess Dido and others fled from her brother Pygmalion, to find a new land to settle in. As colonists they were obviously short of women, for as their ships stopped off at Cyprus to refurbish and take on supplies, they took the opportunity to abduct the temple prostitutes and appoint them as wives. The temple in question would have been in honour of Aphrodite, the goddess of love, who according to legend rose from the foaming sea off Cythera and reappeared in Cyprus fully formed in all her divine beauty. The word Aphrodite means foam born. (Unfortunately this story won't help us find Atlantis, so I will end it here!)

According to the Egyptian priest, the mighty calamity which saw Atlantis slip beneath the waves occurred 9,000 years before the time of Solon—or 9590BC. There is absolutely nothing, in the way of archaeological finds, to indicate even the beginnings of a civilised community in the Mediterranean at this time. All we find are some very primitive hunter gather groups.

Fortunately, greater scholars than I have come to the rescue in this dating problem. Most believe it is simply a copyist's error, perpetrated by an Egyptian priest or scribe whose duty it was to transcribe the papyrus once it had grown old and faded with the years. In this way, 900 could have easily been recorded as 9000. That means if we are now to predate Solon, of 590BC, by 900 years, then it is 1490BC which emerges—a date not that remote from the two set by archaeologists for Thira's eruption, 1500 and 1450. The latter is the more devastating.

If this story told to Solon is the Egyptian recording of that event, then one can imagine refugees coming to Egypt's shore with something either they couldn't explain, or assumed was a war among the gods. The tale would be recorded as the Egyptian priest heard and understood it—difficult in itself, since even the eye witnesses would have had trouble putting it into words. Even then, there would be variations depending on the observer, and where on Crete he was situated at the time of the eruption.

What a wonderful story Thira's big bang became to the young Phaethon, who wanted to drive the sun in his daddy's chariot, yet couldn't handle the horses, and so burnt up everyone on the earth. It would have been quite easy to see the hot ash and pumice falling from the sky in just that way. Then when Zeus got fed up with these antics, he threw a thunderbolt, which missed the target (Phaethon), and instead struck the cone of—guess where, yes—Thira's volcano. There was now a great deluge of water, and only husbandmen, herdsmen, shepherds and those who lived in the mountain survived. How so? If the deluge was of rain, it wouldn't be logical to think of those of the mountains faring any better than those in the cities. If, rather, it was a Tsunamis—a huge wave generated by the eruption—then civic society would have suffered where the hill people did not. With all eruptions, violent rainstorms with thunder and lightning are a common occurrence. Added to and mixed with the rain would be ash. So, initially, it would appear to some that everything was burnt up, while to others there was a great flood from the sea, while yet more experienced a continual muddy rain. After all, how would they know what a Tsunamis was, when even we ourselves didn't until a few years ago!

After the muddy rain, the sky would have darkened with the volume of smoke and ash now floating as dust in the air. Some of the mountain people I suspect were followers of the new god Zeus, and put their survival down to the old gods being vanquished by him. Today this is still remembered as the clash of the Titans, and in Tacitus' time was known as the aggression of Jupiter and Saturn.

Were Noah's people farmers, herdsman and shepherds? According to the Cain and Abel squabble, God wouldn't accept Abel's offering (crops), but would accept Cain's (an animal). This certainly indicates that shepherds were favoured, while tillers of the earthly sod were out of fashion. All one has to ask now is where would we find sheep and shepherds? Most, but not all of the time, sheep like mountain pastures, and as an ex farmer myself I have experienced less trouble with sheep in the hills, where there is a reduced tendency to foot rot (this is brought on by wet lush river meadows). So, is there a chance that Noah's people—the people who were good in God's eyes—lived in the mountains? If they did, then their survival enabled the telling of the tale.

I don't want to get involved in the pros and cons of the Atlantis legend, except where it parallels my theory of the Hebrews as originally Minoans, and the Minoans as the legendary Atlantians. However, for those who wish to do their own research, you will find the account in Plato's *Critias* and *Timaeus*. For those who consider my theory of Atlantis as Crete, or at least as Thira, to be ridiculous, then I am pleased to say that most scholars agree with me that Thira is the most likely model for the legendary Atlantis. For those still not convinced, I suggest a look at Professor J V Luce's book *The End of Atlantis: New Light on an Old Legend*.

We have, I think, gone quite some way to explain the earth burnt up, and the date. But what about the size of Atlantis? According to Plato, the first person there was Evenor, who had a daughter Cleito whom the god Poseidon married. Evenor was a man, which is counter to my preference for Eve, but this does I think get us close. Poseidon, Cleito and their descendants were rulers of various islands in the open sea, and also held sway as far as Egypt and Tyrrhenia. Here is an indication that there were many islands rather than one, towards Greece. If Plato is describing the Mediterranean Sea—and I think he is—then there is only one place today that resembles that location, and that is the Cyclades in the Aegean Sea—with Thira at the middle of it all. According to Plato the island was 3,000 stadia by 2,000. A stadia was 185 metres, or 600 Greek paces, or an eighth of a Roman mile. Three thousand stadia therefore amount to 345 miles, and 2,000 stadia 230 miles.

I am not going to look for an island of these dimensions in the Mediterranean, because there isn't one—nor has there been. What I *am* going to look for is *islands* (plural), because I believe that in the telling of this tale, size did encompass a multiplicity. An atlas of the Aegean will show you many islands whose names end in 'os'. If you measure with a ruler 345 miles, with one end on the south of Crete, and on a north south line, you will find that it covers all the islands ending in 'os', up to the south of Limnos. In fact there is only one island not covered by this—Thasos, a further sixty miles north. There may have been good reason not to include it, in the Atlantian or Minoan domain—since it is only five miles from mainland Greece. The Greece of the Mycenaeans was warlike, desperately trying to learn the sailing skills of the Minoans—skills more in evidence through the legend of Jason and his Argonauts, who could have been present when Thira erupted. Two hundred and thirty miles from the west of Crete are islands whose names also all end in 'os'—except for Rhodes, which anyway was once called Rhodos. Rhodes, similarly, is a mere fifteen miles from the mainland. My conclusion therefore is, if we treat *island* as *islands*, then the area does begin to look like the kingdom of Minos and his Minoans.

Plato goes on to describe the customs, minerals and fruits of Atlantis:

> Also whatever fragrant things there are now in the earth, whether roots, or herbage, or woods or essences which distil from fruits and flowers, grew and thrived in that land, also the fruit which admits cultivation, both the dry sort, which is given up for nourishment and any other which we use for food…and are fruits which spoil with the keeping, and the pleasant kinds of dessert with which we console ourselves after dinner.

Now we have in Genesis 2: 9—

> And out of the ground made the Lord God to grow every tree that is pleasant to the sight, and good for food; the tree of life also in the midst of the garden, and the tree of knowledge of good and evil.

Back to Plato—

The stone which was used in the work they quarried from underneath the centre island. One kind was white, another black and a third red. The entire circuit of the wall...they covered with a coating of brass, the next with tin, and the third which encompassed the citadel flashed with the red light of Orichalcum.

Genesis 2: 12—

And the gold of that land is good: there is bdellium and the onyx stone.

Here are an awful lot of similarities. Orichalcum, according to the dictionary, is a mountain copper or a yellow metal prized by the ancients and often known only by repute, probably a form of brass or a similar alloy. That yellow metal known by repute, I call gold. Again the Bible has bdellium, which is the fragrant resin from a tree. This is reminiscent of those fragrant woods of Atlantis. And is it possible that the white, black and red stone quarried at Atlantis was the onyx of the Bible? If these are only coincidences, then they aren't just one or two—they run throughout the Bible story, the Atlantis legend, and the factual archaeological finds relating to the Minoans.

The Atlantian religion, according to Plato, saw bulls with the run of the temple of Poseidon. The ten kings, being left alone in the temple, after they had offered prayers to the god—that they might capture the victim acceptable to him—hunted the bull, with no more weapons than staves and nooses. The bull they caught they led to the pillar, cutting its throat over it—a pretty tale, Professor Jowett might have said! Except he wasn't alive when archaeologists unearthed the Vapheio cup, which describes in relief the exact scene that Plato has related. This gold cup shows in detail bulls being lured by decoy cows, then captured with ropes, nets and staves. Was this the story of the decoy cow that Theseus brought back concerning Minos's wife? Was the bull becoming prevalent, and the fresco on the walls of Knossos telling the same story as Theseus' legend of the Minotaur? Whatever else

Plato may have said, or given the noble lie to, he could not have told an untruth in this part of his narrative. He couldn't have known about the Vapheio cup, which had been placed underground in a tomb some 800 years before him, and would lie there for almost another 2,500 years after him. In the temple of Poseidon there was a golden statue of the bull in his chariot, drawn by six winged horses and accompanied by a hundred Nereids, riding on dolphins. Nereids were maidens of the sea. One is reminded of the Cherubims, who were angelic figures in Eden. Dolphins were a popular motif on the palace walls at Knossos.

According to Greek mythology, Zeus disguised himself as a white bull and carried Europa, daughter of the king of Sidon (Canaan), off to Crete, where she gave birth to two boys—Minos and Rhadamanthys. They were rewarded for their sense of justice by being made judges of the dead. In this is a Greek legend of Crete in Minos's day, yet it would appear that Minos was a Minoan and possibly an Atlantian. What we have here is the very beginning of the *Olympian* religion, because Thira's eruption put an end to the Minoans and *their* religion (while Minos appears to have been there just before or during this event). From Plato's account, their mutual relations were regulated by the commands of Poseidon, which the law had handed down. They were inscribed by the first kings on a pillar of orichalcum (onyx), and when they were gathered together they consulted about their common interests and inquired if any one of them had transgressed in anything. They passed judgement, and before doing so gave their pledges to one another. Odysseus relates a similar debate amongst the leaders of the Phoenicians, who I have always maintained where migrants from Crete.

The end of Plato's dialogue finishes abruptly, which prompts one to ask was it lost or never written? In finishing, it relates that the attitude of the Atlantians changed:

> And to him who had an eye to see grew visibly debased, for they were losing the fairest of their precious gifts, but to those who had no eye to see the true happiness, they appeared glorious and blessed at the very time when they were

becoming tainted with unrighteous ambition and power. Zeus the god of gods, who ruled according to the law, and was able to see into such things, perceived that an honourable race was in woeful plight, and wanting to inflict punishment upon them—that they may be chastened and improve—collected all the gods into their most holy habitation, which being placed in the centre of the world beheld all created things. And when he had collected them together, he spoke as follows...

Plato's narrative ends there, but what do you think Zeus said? Well, here's what the Hebrew God said in Genesis 6: 5 8—

And God saw that the wickedness of man was great in the earth, and that every imagination of the thoughts of his heart was only evil continually. And it repented the Lord that he had made man on the earth, and it grieved him at his heart. And the Lord said, I will destroy man whom I have created from the face of the earth; both man, and beast, and the creeping thing, and the fowls of the air; for it repenteth me that I have made him. But Noah found grace in the eyes of the Lord.

We don't know what Zeus did or said, but we do know that the whole point of the Atlantis story is its supposed disappearance under the waves, the deluge—which could only have been brought about by Zeus's wrath. There is another legend that is Greek—not biblical, or Minoan, or Atlantian—which tells of Zeus, the king of the gods, resolved to destroy humanity by means of a flood. Deucalion constructed an ark in which, according to one version, he and his wife rode it out and landed on Mt Parnassus, in southern Greece. Something tells me—and I hope it tells you—that these two narratives are more than coincidentally similar. What Zeus says is what God says in Genesis 6: 7—

And the Lord said, I will destroy man whom I have created from the face of the earth...

Before closing on Atlantis, I would just like to throw one more large spanner in the works by recording what *Colliers Encyclopaedia* has to say. Vol 6, p106: 'A favourite theory is that the biblical paradise of Eden is located in Atlantis.'

Now *Colliers* is not going to record any old lopsided theory in an encyclopaedia if it doesn't have scholarly authenticity—though what I *don't* know is what has brought scholars to this conclusion: except one just has to see the similarities threading their way through both legends.

All we can say now is, was Minoan Crete the legendary Atlantis? I have told you all I know, but I do believe this to be the best theory so far advanced, and clearly it has my vote of confidence. Now it's your turn. Put your knowledge and imagination to work.

What can you come up with?

Before I close, I have just found a series of books called *Milestones in History*, published by the Readers' Digest organisation. There is an edition on ancient empires, with a chapter entitled 'The Eruption of Santorini, 1450BC', which commences with the words, 'The legend of Atlantis...' So, again, I'm not the only one to think of it in this way—it seems many already accept it as the true Atlantis.

Ask Moses

Scholars and archaeologists have been looking for Moses for 2,000 years, so asking him if his ancestral blood is that of the Minoans isn't a practical proposition. Yet there just might be something that's been missed, simply because no one has thought of associating Moses with the Minoans. In fact when certain archaeological items were unearthed by Sir William Flinders Petrie, the Minoan civilisation hadn't yet been discovered. Petrie found pottery on a site at Gurob in Egypt that puzzled him. Years later, when Minoan pottery had been classified— as a new and unique form peculiar only to itself—Petrie's find was seen to belong to that group—but in the meantime there were other puzzling facts. The people linked to these artefacts, whoever they where, kept themselves to themselves, had their own weights and measures, and were not in good health. Moreover when they left their village, they left in a hurry. The village in question is certainly of the right period for Moses, and bears all the hallmarks of involvement with the exodus.

One thing we know from the Bible about Moses is that he was found by Pharaoh's daughter Thermuthis, afloat in a basket of bulrushes somewhere on the river Nile. She took him in and adopted him as her own son. Why Moses had been given up to the Nile was this: Pharaoh had decreed all male children of the Israelites in Egypt were to be slain:

And he [Pharaoh] said, When ye do the office of a midwife
to the Hebrew women, and see them upon the stools [these

were special seats for sitting on to give birth]; if it be a son, then ye shall kill him: but if it be a daughter, then she shall live. (Exodus 1: 16)

It was because of this that the mother of Moses hid him in a basket of bulrushes and set him on the Nile—so this is as good a place as any to set about establishing Moses' birth.

I myself sat by the Nile, and watched a clump of reeds float by. From that I timed the appearance of the next clump, and from this was able to calculate that the Nile flowed at about two and a half miles an hour, or walking pace. I was at Luxor, or ancient Thebes, the capital of the Ramesses pharaohs. My hotel, the Sonesta St George, was about two kilometres south, or upriver from the great temple complexes of Karnak, and one kilometre from Thebes. If Pharaoh's wife was to find Moses adrift on the Nile, it stood to reason she was either at Thebes or Karnak, and that Moses had been set on the water not far from where I sat. Now of course I may have been romanticising.

Who was this pharaoh who wanted to kill off Israel's male issue, and why should he want to do such a terrible thing? To these questions the Bible gives a clue.

We know that the Hebrews entered Egypt at Joseph's invitation, as this was part of Pharaoh's reward for Joseph. We read in Exodus (1: 7): 'And the children of Israel were fruitful, and increased abundantly, and multiplied, and waxed exceeding mighty; and the land was filled with them.' Exodus (1: 8) tells us: 'Now there arose up a new king over Egypt, which knew not Joseph.'

It is written that Joseph was thirty when he stood before Pharaoh, and died at the age of 110. Therefore Joseph was in Egypt eighty years. One pharaoh to have reigned for long enough to witness much of that span was Ramesses II, whose era was 1304 1237BC (some sixty seven years). It is also possible that Joseph arrived in Egypt in Seti I's reign, 1318 1304BC. From 1318 to 1237 is a period of eighty one years, and probably a better candidate—especially since it might have taken Joseph fourteen or fifteen years to earn Pharaoh's reward, the Hebrew influx into Egypt.

Why did Joseph get a reward in the first place? It was because he had told Pharaoh that there would be seven good years followed by seven lean. I think we can say with some justification that to earn the reward he would have had to see those fourteen years out—just the length of time before Ramesses II came to the throne. However, there is something else which indicates the time of Joseph's arrival in Egypt. Seti I was beginning to experience raids on Egypt by a mysterious race of people known as the Sea People. If we read in the Bible of Joseph when he first exercised authority in Egypt, we see that Jacob sent Joseph's brothers into Egypt to buy corn. When they arrived, they met up with this man in authority, who recognised them as his brothers. Genesis (42: 30): The man [Joseph], who is the lord of the land [Egypt], spake roughly to us, and took us for spies of the country.' Joseph had only just been promoted. He had not yet proved his worth to Pharaoh, and so had not yet been rewarded. Yet here it is being suggested that there were spies in the country. Why would Egypt be worried at this, and constantly on the lookout? Perhaps because all wasn't well on the frontiers, and Seti's concern at these raids was serious.

A thing about spies is that they tend to indicate a war is about to begin, and an invasion possible. People have to be on the lookout for strangers wandering about. Anyone who looks, dresses or speaks differently is an automatic suspect. So here perhaps is evidence that an invasion or war was imminent. Now if, in 1940, a Welshman or a Scotsman had talked to you in his native tongue, and traditionally attired, you wouldn't necessarily have reported the fact—these things being foreign but familiar. So for Joseph's brothers to be stopped very probably indicates that whatever their characteristics were, they didn't appear to be Egyptian or of their neighbours the Canaanites. This leads me to believe that the Hebrews, if not new in the land of Canaan, weren't that numerous. Their dress may have been unfamiliar, if their hairstyle was not (it looked very much like that worn by the Libyans, who were definitely part of the confederation of Sea People). The Sea People or Libyans seemed then to have come from nowhere, though to us it is almost certain that they originally came from Crete.

Again there is this distinctive hairstyle that both the Libyans and Jews adopted (the Jews still wear it today), and it was definitely Minoan. We know this from Minoan wall paintings, and as seen in the Egyptian tombs of the nobles of Tuthmosis III's reign (1479 1425). Here we see envoys of the Keftiu bringing gifts to Pharaoh—scenes of a people that never appeared again.

The Sea People also caused trouble in the time of Ramesses II, and when his son Merenptah succeeded to the throne, something decisive had to be done. Merenptah must have been the pharaoh in Exodus 1: 8, 'which knew not Joseph', and this is the pharaoh I consider to have caused Moses to be cast upon the Nile in his basket of bulrushes. This is I know contentious, because this is where most scholars will now disagree with me. For most learned bodies, it was Pharaoh Merenptah who was involved in the exodus, and at first glance this would appear to be likely. Sir Flinders Petrie, digging in Egypt in around 1885, found the only monument which mentioned the Hebrews—and this had been erected by Merenptah. A part of its inscription has been deciphered as follows:

> Devastated is Libya, Hittites are quiet, Canaan...Isiriar [Israel] is laid waste without seed, Palestine...

What does 'without seed' imply, since only males have it?

Another argument in favour of Merenptah as pharaoh of the exodus is the discovery of salt in his mummified remains, suggesting he had drowned at sea. My counter argument is, there were scuffles with opportunist Sea People on and off from Sethos I's reign right through to Ramesses III's. Like the Saxons and Vikings, they were raiding parties, whose skirmishes were largely uncoordinated—until Ramesses III, when the real battle for survival took place. At that point the Sea People had come to conquer and settle. During Merenptah's reign he retaliated, sending a reprisal expedition into Palestine, which seems to have laid waste the Hebrews. Initially we might well interpret Exodus as the Hebrews leaving Egypt in Merenptah's reign, but this doesn't seem consistent if Merenptah was in Palestine laying waste to the

Israelites, who couldn't very well have arrived before him. However, it is now known that there were, at this time, Hebrews living in Palestine who had never been into Egypt. The Ashmolean Museum has it that the Old Testament's account of Joshua's conquest suggests that in central Palestine—particularly around Shechem—there was already a settled a group of Hebrews who had never been in Egypt, and had not taken part in the exodus. Moreover they had established themselves here in the fourteenth century BC. So, this 'laying waste' *could* refer to them, just as easily as it implies the killing off of new born male children issuing from those Hebrews already living in Egypt, and the birth of Moses.

Why do this to a peaceful people living in your land? Exodus (1: 7): 'And the children of Israel were fruitful, and increased abundantly, and multiplied, and waxed exceeding mighty; and the land was filled with them.' Was it because the Hebrews appeared to be consorting with the Sea People, the enemies of Egypt? Exodus (1: 10): 'Come on [this is what the Israelite thinks Pharaoh is saying to the Egyptians], let us deal wisely with them [the Israelites]; lest they multiply, and it come to pass, that, when there falleth out any war, they join also unto our enemies, and fight against us, and so get them up out of the land.' Here in the Bible is evidence that Egypt had enemies and that the Israelites were thinking of joining forces with them—a reason why Merenptah would want to act as he did. With the male population of the Hebrews expunged, so too would the seed of the Hebrews disappear. Of necessity, the remaining females must then marry into Egyptian stock.

Now to the salt in Merenptah's body. This is easily explained. Firstly there would have been large quantities of natron salts used in the mummification process, although this is not the kind of salt referred to—rather sea salt. Sand, with a presence of sea salt, was used to fill out the body cavities, prior to wrapping the corpse. It so happens that on re examination, there are other pharaohs where such deposits of sea salt were found. From this we can deduce that *these* pharaohs died in the delta region, where sand from the beaches was easily available. People who died further upriver had the benefit of desert sand, which by its nature was devoid of both microscopic marine life and any particles of salt. Furthermore Merenptah's mummy showed no evidence of drowning or a violent death.

Ramesses II was an old man when Merenptah laid waste the Hebrews, in 1227BC—this was three years before Merenptah came to the throne. Ramesses, as the one who knew Joseph, and who wasn't yet dead, couldn't have been the culprit. However, my most important point is this—that if the Israelites had left Egypt in 1227, they would have had thirty six years in which to establish themselves in Palestine. Yet all agree that when Ramesses III threw out the Sea People for the last time in c1186BC, these latter—unvanquished and undaunted—turned away from Egypt and themselves moved into Palestine, conquering all as they went. If the Hebrews had been there when the Sea People arrived, they would not have been strong enough to withstand their ferocity. After all, it was they who had been prepared to take on the might of Egypt. The Hebrews would have found themselves swallowed up, and thereafter we might never have heard of them. So, no—the Hebrews under Judas migrated into Palestine as a friendly tribe among the Sea People confederation. It should also be remembered that it was in Palestine that the Danaans, also among that confederation, amalgamated with the Hebrews and became the tribe of Dan. This could only have happened in the reign of Ramesses III. Therefore Merenptah must have been the one wanting to kill off all Hebrew new born males—in the year 1227BC.

If Moses was alive in 1191, when, I suggest, the exodus took place—then this was in the reign of Ramesses III. This would have made Moses thirty six when he led his Hebrews into Palestine—not young or old, but mature enough to face the desert before entering his promised land. To complicate matters, there where two exoduses from Egypt, at roughly the same time. Both are recorded in the Bible in Exodus, but appear as one. Tacitus also mentions the two exodi. The Judas migration moved into northern Palestine, forming the kingdom of Judaea, and I feel it is these Hebrews who were consorting with the enemies of Pharaoh. There are those who say that the destruction of Israel signifies that the Israelites were already in Palestine, and that the exodus had already taken place. I would agree that indeed they were—although these Hebrews, or Hapiru, had never been in Egypt in the first place. In the Ashmolean, the book *Archaeology, Artefacts and the Bible*, by P R S Moorey, shows in the twelfth century BC catastrophic disruption of settled urban life by migrant or dissident peoples, among whom Israelites, Aramaeans and the Sea People formed a distinguishable element. This is the exodus of Judas. What could be confusing is that in c1425BC the diplomatic archives of Pharaoh Amenophis III include correspondence with the local Canaanite rulers, which reveals considerable political instability with recurrent internal feuding, persistent strife, and marauding bands of Hapiru.

The earlier mention of the Hapiru has nothing to do with the exodus out of Egypt as it is far too early, but it does show the emergence of a new disruptive, landless race of people. I think it is here that the refugees from Thira's eruption came ashore in Canaan creating unrest. This is the Exodus of Noah.

Interestingly the biblical story is similar, except that it is God who brought the disease on the Egyptians. Whether or not this was true, the Bible, or specifically Leviticus, clearly states that the Hebrews did have leprosy. Whether they had it when they left Egypt, we don't know—though they had got it when they were in the desert. Somehow I don't think this is where they caught it. So, whose version is correct? Generally if you're writing the history of your own people, you're not over eager to admit that you were exiled from one of the most bountiful lands in the known world, as carriers of disease. That Moses led these people out of Egypt is without doubt, since as testament to that we have a Jewish historian, a rabbi of high birth, a supporter of doctrine laid down by Moses—namely Josephus Flavius. It was he who also translated and preserved the ancient Egyptian *List of Kings* and their histories, as written and recorded by the Egyptian priest Manetho, in the third century BC. Manetho had been commissioned by Pharaoh Ptolemy to write it. Ptolemy was a Greek, and a descendant of one of Alexander the Great's generals, also called Ptolemy (who took over Egypt on the death of Alexander). So, all the Ptolemys and

Cleopatras were in reality Greek, with no knowledge of Egypt's past or language. Manetho was one of the last priests able to read the ancient hieroglyphs and translate them into Greek.

In the book of Leviticus, this is clearly giving the Jews something to worry about. One could say that Leviticus was the medical journal of the Israelites, the do's and don'ts so to speak of daily life. It covers such interesting topics as adultery to lying down with animals. Leviticus also records what you have to do to cleanse yourself, or the punishments (including death) for those over zealous in their love of animals. There are also some fifty odd verses, for the priests to read (Chapters 13 to 14), devoted to a primitive diagnosis of leprosy. Leviticus (13: 2): 'When a man shall have in the skin of his flesh a rising, a scab, or bright spot, and it be in the skin of his flesh like the plague of leprosy; then he shall be brought unto Aaron the priest, or unto one of his sons the priests.' One can sense their desperation as they tried to find a cure.

I truly believe that what you are reading in these chapters is not myth at all, but actually took place. In 14:14 we have the ceremony that will bring about a cure: 'And the priest shall take some of the blood of the trespass offering, and the priest shall put it upon the tip of the right ear of him that is to be cleansed, and upon the thumb of his right hand, and upon the great toe of his right foot.' I can feel their terrible fear, their hopelessness as they perform this ceremony, for of course this could never be a cure. It was a last ditch attempt to give some hope to those who suffered. From this, interestingly, we can possibly conclude that Moses was right handed. I have discussed this with left handed people, and discovered that if they were to think up such a ceremony, it would undoubtedly be sinistral (i.e., would have a left hand orientation).

In 22: 4 it would appear that Aaron's two sons were now suspected of having the disease: 'What man soever of the seed of Aaron is a leper, or hath a running issue; he shall not eat of the holy things, until he be clean.' Aaron and his sons were priests, and as such were allowed to eat of the sacrifice. I suspect there were many Israelites suffering from leprosy, as I suspect from this verse that Aaron and his sons had developed running sores. Leviticus 8: 23 tells us: 'And he slew it [the sacrificial ram]; and Moses took of the blood of it, and put it upon the tip of Aaron's right ear, and upon the thumb of his right hand, and upon the great toe of his right foot.' This, the hoped for cure, was now being administered by Moses himself, the top man—and surely one can say if the highest ministers were getting leprosy, then it must have been rife among the rest of the tribe. Verse 24 reads: 'And he [Moses] brought Aaron's sons, and Moses put of the blood upon the tip of their right ear, and upon the thumbs of their right hands, and upon the great toes of their right feet: and Moses sprinkled the blood upon the altar round about.' Later, in 16:1, we learn: 'And the Lord spake unto Moses after the death of the two sons of Aaron, when they offered before the Lord, and died'—from which I think it is clear that Aaron's two sons died but Aaron seems to have survived.

If one reads further into Leviticus, it will be noticed that the sacrifice or offering that had to be made on behalf of someone suspected of having leprosy, took the form of a much more interesting menu. No longer did the Lord (or really the priests) want a *burnt* offering. Whatever was sacrificed had, in the end, to be edible. Chapter 2: 7 is quite specific about this: 'And if thy oblation be a meat offering baken in the fryingpan, it shall be made of fine flour with oil.' This indicates to me that many sacrifices were now taking place, and the old tradition of barbecued leg of lamb had become unacceptable.

Leviticus was written while the Israelites were still in the desert, under Moses—and as I have said, I don't think it was here that they contracted leprosy. The desert is not the sort of place where one would expect it to arise, due to the lack of water and general sterility. Egypt, with its abundant water supply—the Nile—and a large population packed together on a narrow strip of fertile land, would have been much more likely to breed the disease. This can only mean that the Israelites were affected before leaving Egypt. Certainly when they got to the desert, Moses forbade the eating of swine. Leviticus (11: 7 8): 'And the swine, though he divide the hoof, and be clovenfooted, yet he cheweth not the cud; he is unclean to you. Of their flesh shall ye not eat, and their carcass shall ye not touch; they are unclean to you.'

Was Moses now of the view that swine and leprosy went hand in hand? In Egypt's hot climate, without refrigeration, I would go along with the idea that pork and man don't travel well.

So far Moses hasn't told us the origin of his people. They had obviously been refugees in Mesopotamia, before going down into Egypt under Joseph—but refugees from where? They couldn't have sprung from just nowhere, but wherever they *had* come from, they couldn't return. When conquerors came, they would either slay all the inhabitants or kill off the males and marry the females. Males in any clan would fight to the death, to retain their territorial rights.

Moses has given us Egypt as a place where his people for the first time put down roots, not for a couple of years, but for eighty. Given that span, it might just be possible for archaeologists to find remnants of their possessions, a record of their passing. It was with this in mind that in 1888 the British Museum asked Sir William Flinders Petrie to carry out archaeological excavations in Egypt, to try to substantiate what was written in the Bible on the early history of the Hebrews. Apart from the Stela set up by Merenptah, concerning the destruction of the seed of Israel, he found nothing to indicate the presence of the Hebrews in Egypt—or did he?

Petrie had been digging at Kahun, but by accident also started digging at the nearby ancient village at Gurob. From A R David's book, *Ancient Egypt*, it is apparent that the workmen there kept themselves to themselves. Their religious practices, as well as their weights and measures, were different from those of the Egyptians. At this stage it can be concluded, tentatively, that the foreign residents may have come from a number of areas, including Syria, Palestine, and the Aegean Islands, and that they may have come as traders, itinerant workers or perhaps originally as prisoners of war. However, the quantity, range and type of articles left at the site seem to indicate a more sudden and unpremeditated evacuation. A perfectly good wooden trowel had been left behind, still with plaster on it. An unusual number of medical instruments were found, implying a peculiarly high incidence of medical problems. A 'more sudden and unpremeditated evacuation' reminds me of Exodus (12: 39): 'And they baked unleavened cakes of the dough which they brought forth out of Egypt, for it was not leavened; because they were thrust out of Egypt, and could not tarry, neither had they prepared for themselves any victual.' That they were 'thrust out' coincides with Tacitus, *and* with Petrie's discovery.

What was Mycenaean pottery doing up the Nile, an appreciable distance from the delta? When I eventually acquired the book by Petrie, *Seventy Years of Archaeology*, my heart dropped, because in it he states that the village of Kahun had been laid out in the twelfth dynasty (the eleventh and twelfth dynasties were 2040 1640). This had been done for the workmen building Sesostris II's tomb, c1800BC. At first glance this blew my theory of an association with Crete, because the twelfth dynasty was well before Thira's eruption. Fortunately, it was while Petrie was digging here that he accidentally came on another workers' village at Gurob, and goes on: 'At Gurob the foreign connection was of special interest. For the first time Mycenaean pottery was found in place in Egypt, and so completely mixed up with the remains of the end of the eighteenth dynasty as to date it decisively.... To be able to step back to 1400BC and firmly link Aegean archaeology was a decisive gain.'

Petrie was perplexed, because although he considered the pottery he had found to be Mycenaean, it seemed not quite to be so. His colleagues, Reinach and Evans, confirmed his doubts, when in their view it was Aegean—that was, older than Mycenaean. Aegean style pottery is of course Minoan, but in Petrie's time Sir Arthur Evans had not yet unearthed this new civilisation on Crete. As a consequence this intricate pottery dug up around the Aegean took that as its name, simply because no one knew where it had originated.

The end of the eighteenth dynasty was in fact 1319BC. At some point around 1290, Joseph came down into Egypt, while by 1224 the Hebrews were receiving rough treatment at the hands of the Egyptians. By my calculations, Moses was leaving Egypt in about 1191BC. As for the pottery, A R David states, 'Tests...were carried out, to see if it was made by the workers themselves, or whether it was imported, but no firm evidence emerged to say that it was. However, I would add to this, no other pottery has been found of this style.' If pottery *had* been imported, then it stands to reason you wouldn't travel 150 miles upriver before selling. You would start selling as soon as you arrived, at the port of entry, then slowly move inland as you began to saturate those opening markets. Therefore it stands to reason that samples would have turned up at other sites—yet they don't. That being the case, it looks as though the people were making their own, in the same traditional way as their ancestors before them.

What these workers were doing at Gurob, we don't know—but if the village was made for them then we must look nearby for signs of their activities. Were they engaged with the tomb that the workers from Kahun had been building over 500 years before (though in their case robbing it)? Graffiti has been found showing that Ramesses II sanctioned just that order of plunder—masonry removed from Sesostris' tomb and shipped down the Nile, for the construction of Pi Ramesses in the delta. This was the very place where the Hebrews were labouring. At the same time one can say that whoever was working at Gurob was also indirectly employed on the building of Pi Ramesses. Petrie discovered three stone blocks incorporated in it which he confirmed as originally part of Sesostris' tomb. Could it be that here was the second group of Hebrews under Moses supplying purloined materials to the delta group under Judas?

Pi Ramesses took some years to build. Although begun by Ramesses II, its construction could quite easily have extended into Merenptah's time, and even beyond. At any stage during this period the Hebrews could have worked on this site. And of course, as A R David has said, workers at Gurob may well have been prisoners of war, from the Aegean, whose inclination was to stick together, albeit under supervision. If that was so, one intriguing question is, would they have been allowed to keep their own weights, measures and religion? If they hadn't been in Egypt that long, they wouldn't yet have adjusted to the Egyptian way of life. One must bear in mind also that the Jewish religion is one of the longest running, open to few if any changes. If they *had* been prisoners of war, taken in Ramesses II's time, they would have come from Palestine, and could therefore have been descendants of refugees from Minoan Crete, who had come ashore in Canaan. So why didn't Petrie make more of this pottery? The answer is simple. In AD1888 every schoolboy knew that the Hebrews had originated in Mesopotamia. The last thing Petrie would have thought of was a connection between the Hebrews and Crete—Sir Arthur Evans' finds on Minoan Crete still a thing of the future.

'Ask Moses' is the heading for this chapter, so I *am* going to ask him:

'Moses, were you ever at a place called Gurob, a most beautiful and fertile part of Egypt, 150 miles up the Nile—possibly the same area that Pharaoh gave Joseph?'

Genesis (45: 18): 'And [Pharaoh said] take your father and your households, and come unto me; and I will give you the good of the land of Egypt, and ye shall eat the fat of the land.'

If, Moses, you weren't, then someone with problems similar to yours, was. Someone with connections in Minoan Crete.

I think for all the suggestion that the Hebrews were asking Pharaoh to let them go, they were still required to leave in a hurry. For the Judas group, this was because they consorted with Pharaoh's enemies, and for the Moses group because of leprosy. Exodus (16: 3): 'And the children of Israel said unto them [Moses and Aaron], Would to God we had died by the hand of the Lord in the land of Egypt, when we sat by the flesh pots, and when we did eat bread to the full; for ye have brought us forth into this wilderness, to kill this whole assembly with hunger'—which seems to confirm Tacitus' account. Note that they say 'by the hand of the Lord' and not 'by the hand of Pharaoh'. Was the Lord killing them with leprosy? And why in heaven's name should they want to consort with Pharaoh's enemies, when they had been befriended by the Egyptians and were living off the fat of the land? Exodus (1: 7): 'And the children of Israel were fruitful, and increased abundantly, and multiplied, and waxed exceeding mighty; and the land was filled with them.'

It wasn't that they considered Pharaoh a hard taskmaster, because he wasn't that till he discovered they'd betrayed him to his enemies. It wasn't because, on a whim, they decided to join with the invaders, because in theory neither party had met before. So—why bite the hand that had fed you? Why make an enemy of those who had taken you in and given you refuge? There can be only one answer. The invaders and the Hebrews discovered they were kinsfolk (for I consider their hairstyles gave them the clue). Here were people the Hebrews could trust to give them land of their own, in Egypt. This was their incentive, and it outweighed any loyalty they might have felt towards Egypt.

In all fairness I consider Moses played no part in this. This was all of Judas's doing. After Ramesses III beat off, in 1186, the invasion of the Sea People, the Hebrews under Judas saw the light, and knowing there was no place for them in Egypt now, took the opportunity to leave with the other tribes—the Philistines, the Danaans, etc.

I don't think the Israelites in the delta, under Judas, or Moses farther south, crossed the Red Sea. Some scholars say this was really the Reed Sea, which seems a big step to take. The word 'red' does at first glance seem easily derived from 'reed', but this would have been written in Hebrew, in which language I am not so sure of the similarity between the two. However, I do consider the Israelites under Judas, and with the Sea People, were actively fighting Pharaoh in 1186BC. We know that Ramesses trapped the confederation of all the Sea People in the swampy ground in the delta—a place abundant in reeds. As Ramesses' monument proclaims:

> I prepared the river mouth [Nile] like a strong wall with warships, galleys and light craft. They were completely equipped both fore and aft with brave fighters carrying their weapons, and infantry of all the pick of Egypt, being like a roaring lion in the mountains, chariots with able warriors and goodly officers whose hands were competent. A net was prepared for them to ensnare them, those who entered into the river mouth being confined and fallen within it, pinioned in their places, butchered and their corpses hacked up.... As for those that reached my boundary, their seed is not. Their hearts and souls are finished unto all eternity.

For those who escaped, flight was eastward into Palestine, and this I consider was the Exodus of Judas. The biblical account of God parting the sea and bringing down on the Egyptians plague and pestilence, seems quite at odds with what archaeological research has suggested. This is not to impugn the Bible, for what it implies is that whoever won the war wrote their own history. If the Hebrews *didn't* win, they did migrate east, and lived to fight and write another day. The Bible is a book full of wisdom and learning, acquired over thousands of years. Only when it's taken as gospel, as unassailable truth, does prejudice and false prophecy spring up, dousing its pages with fear in the face of God.

It would appear that Moses took no part in the liaison with Pharaoh's enemies. It seems reasonable then that his group would not have been looked upon as kindred spirits in that fight against that Pharaoh. Consequently, it makes sense that Moses would wander in the desert for forty years until he felt it safe to be accepted into this new Canaan, this Palestine, this new home of the Philistines. Even so, he had to form his own kingdom—at first not a part of the kingdom of Judaea. We can see this happening from the Bible, as Moses tells his people whom they can negotiate with, whom they must leave alone, and whom they can fight. Even then, they're instructed to wait until the warriors of these tribes have died of old age. Deuteronomy (2: 16 19): 'So it came to pass, when all the men of war were consumed and dead from among the people, that the Lord spake unto me, saying, Thou art to pass over through Ar, the coast of Moab, this day: and when thou comest nigh over against the children of Ammon, distress them not, nor meddle with them: for I will not give thee of the land of the children of Ammon any possession; because I have given it unto the children of Lot for a possession.' Again, in Deuteronomy (2: 4 5): 'And command thou the people, saying, Ye are to pass through the coast of your brethren the children of Esau, which dwell in Seir; and they shall be afraid of you: take ye good heed unto yourselves therefore: meddle not with them; for I will not give you of their land, not so much as a foot breadth…' This is a possible reason why Moses kept his people in the desert for forty years, away from all the strife taking place in

Palestine, what with the Sea People fighting for the lands of the resident owners. Moses' people were waiting for the old warriors either to die off or grow too old and enfeebled. Nevertheless, I suspect the Philistines did not take kindly to this incursion, and although the Danaans teamed up with Moses (becoming the tribe of Dan) the Philistines became their enemy.

The *New Encyclopaedia Britannica* states that the Philistines came from Caphtor, possibly Crete. Deuteronomy 2: 23 calls them 'Caphtorims, which came forth out of Caphtor...' Jeremiah 47: 4 says '...for the lord will spoil the Philistines, the remnant of the country of Caphtor.' In about 1200BC the Philistines took over the southern coastal plains of Palestine, just prior to the Jews' arrival there (I consider they arrived at the same time under Judas, but later under Moses). Palestine was named after them, and they were one of the Sea People. The 'remnant of Caphtor' would seem to indicate that there was some devastation on Crete—for remember too that the Philistines were driven out of Egypt at approximately the time the Israelites left. They came into conflict with each other only through disputes over land rights in Canaan—but how did the Bible know this? Why, evidently, did the Israelites have more knowledge of the Mediterranean peoples than of Mesopotamia? Could it be that they too were part of this history?

Did Moses know that God had made Thira erupt and forced the population to migrate? He must have known the story of Noah—this preceded him. He certainly knew about the Caphtorims, who came out of Caphtor (or Crete). The story tallies with the archaeological evidence put forward by Sir Arthur Evans, with his newly discovered civilisation of the Minoans. From this brief mention it could be said that the God of Moses had caused this. In which case here is a direct link. For how did or why should Moses or God know about the history of the Cretans, when at that time in history the Hebrews were supposed to be in Mesopotamia? It must not be forgotten that according to the official Hebrew version, they *had* originated in Mesopotamia, and had never been near Canaan before. So how was it that they knew, or even *bothered* to know about Crete?

Adding to this, in P H Newby's book, *Fighting Warrior Pharaohs*, it is said that they (the Philistines) came by sea from Crete, a land the Israelites were so convinced was the Philistines' homeland that they called the Negeb where they settled the *Cretan South*.

I am reminded of what the *Encyclopaedia Britannica* has to say. Between 1375 and 1350BC Minoan power collapsed. The reasons are not exactly clear, but it is possible that natural causes—such as an earthquake and tidal wave (Tsunamis)—were partly responsible, although further Mycenaean invasions also may have been responsible (due to the chaos caused by the earthquakes). Whatever the details, it appears that the collapse of the Minoan and Mycenaean cultures touched off a number of mass migrations of the so called Sea People. This toppled the Hittite Empire in Anatolia, menaced Egypt, and changed the entire course of the Near East. One of the most important of these migrations consisted of two Aegean peoples known in history as the Philistines and the Danites, who threatened the Nile delta of Egypt during the reign of Pharaoh Ramesses III (c1194 1162BC). They were finally repulsed, and sailed east to settle on the coast that bears their name: Palestine. The Philistines continually warred with the Hebrew tribes, but the Danites split off, moved inland and eventually joined with the Hebrews, contributing the tribe of Dan. However, according to seismologists, the two eruptions of Thira were in 1500 and 1450BC, about a hundred years earlier than shown in the *Encyclopaedia*.

Leprosy, according to my *Colliers Encyclopaedia*, is a very old disease which dates back to the Old Testament. Only five to ten per cent of those exposed to it ever develop it in full, and it takes anything from two to twenty years for it to become evident to the victim that he or she has it. It cannot be incubated by artificial means, and it is not contagious through touch—it is transmitted by inhaling the spores through the nose or mouth. Given these facts, how was it that Moses and the Israelites were rife with it? To me, if most of Moses' people had it, it can only mean that they had been living together for a considerable time. But if the spores are ingested via the nose or mouth, how could this have occurred? The desert winds of Egypt would have been relatively sterile, so if a large number of people had the disease then it is probable they caught it in the same place—moreover a place not that well aerated. Could Sesostris II's tomb have been that confined place, where some contagious disease had lain in wait for 550 years? That could explain why those workers at Kahun 500 years earlier had made 'a more sudden and unpremeditated evacuation', leaving behind those spores for those who would come later. As this later generation of unknowing workers dug themselves into the bowels of this confined tomb, lifting and shifting, is it possible they were perspiring and breathing heavily? It has always intrigued me as to why Egyptologists wear medical masks when entering a newly opened tomb. Were the Hebrews unknowingly afflicted with the curse of Pharaoh Sesostris II? Could Moses have been an overseer of this place? Could that Aegean or Minoan pottery have been theirs? There's a lot of 'coulds' in my theory but in mitigation there's too many coincidences to throw out this line of enquiry. After all, do we want future Egyptologists sitting there twiddling their thumbs? It's only right we old ones should give them something to think about!

Ask Moses! Well, I consider I have, *and* that he's answered many of my questions. Yet he is still saying to me, 'Look once more at Gurob—with a different approach, and a different understanding. Then you might just find me.'

From the Future to the Past

*I*t seems to be the vogue for scholars to write books on history at the point where that subject and science fiction merge. I'm afraid I cannot myself subscribe to this. Of course, I believe there are living creatures out there in distant space, for we are living proof that that can happen. I can even believe that some super creature could evolve and travel at the speed of light to our own tiny planet. What I can't believe is that they came and went without leaving behind any visible sign of their visit. All we have is what archaeologists can show as the natural progress of evolution.

So no, I don't believe that the Egyptians, the Mayas cum Aztec, or the Incas evolved from some super race which some have associated with the mysterious Atlantians. As Professor John Roper has said, for this to happen the Atlantians had first to cross to Egypt, then take two thousand years for the Egyptians to take this so called common culture to Mexico. The truth of it seems to me quite simple: if one culture can develop an idea, why can't another? Why should it not be the case that two distinct and separate peoples independently develop the pyramid? Especially as there was a common denominator—namely that all encompassing sun. Everyone must have looked at the sun at some time, and wondered. The sun takes its message around the world not in a thousand years but in twenty four hours, and has done this every day for millions of years. So, it is easy to imagine every type of people trying to find a way of getting at it.

Yet in saying all this I have two little snippets of puzzling information, which could quite easily verge on the science fiction scene. As I have already mentioned, I have done my travelling into Peru in search of the Incas. I have seen the way they cut their stone. No gaps, not even room to slip a credit card between the slabs, and not a grain of cement to fuse them. Yet in many cases the stones or boulders had been shaped to many facets and angles in order to accommodate the stones abutting them. These must have been worked time and again in order to achieve the perfect fit. Even more puzzling, they would cut row after row of stones, all identical in shape, then for no apparent reason get a large boulder and make these rows fit into it. The most famous stone in Cuzco has some thirty six angles. Whatever else they were famous for, of which gold and silver appear top of the list, we should not forget their stonework, a miracle of craftsmanship which has long since died out. Had I ever seen work like it? Well, yes—and the puzzle was, where it was, and why it was.

I was walking along Hadrian's Wall and had arrived at Birdoswald, once a great military fort on the northernmost limits of the Roman empire. I wasn't looking at anything particular, and was more intent on breathing in the very atmosphere of the place, trying to get some idea of what it must have been like when new, and the legions keen and unconquerable. I could quite visualise that time when Rome finally lost its communications with this wild frontier. I could understand the confusion of the soldiers who were stationed here, when supplies and the pay chest ceased to arrive. I could almost see them take matters into their own hands, as some set off to find their homeland, while others turned to tilling the soil or brigandage. I reviewed this ancient wall. Walls were all the same, from one end of the Roman empire to the other. Nice, rough cut stones as facing masonry, about nine inches by nine, with a good dollop of cement around and between—the sort of craftsmanship that can be seen in the wall of Roman London. Then I stopped, for there on the west gate (or it could have been the east gate), right down in the bottom courses, were two lines of masonry. Now where had I seen that before? Dear me, if it wasn't in Peru! The stones were all dressed and smooth. They'd been cut to fit into other stones, which had been cut to fit into them. There was not a grain of cement in these two rows, which were about fifteen feet long. Of course, I took out my credit card, and applied the final test—and no, I couldn't slip it in anywhere. As for cutting these angles, there was no rhyme or reason to it. The whole thing could have been put up quicker if they'd just lopped off the odd angles of stone to make a rough square. As for cement, this was evident in the stonework before these stones were laid, and even to the left and right and on the courses above. So, whoever it was who laid these stones had done so as a sample, and because it must have been time consuming he was obviously taken off the job. To add to my misery there was a plaque stating that these two courses were the finest stonework to be found on the entire wall. So where in heaven's name did our stonemason come from? If he was that good he'd never have been a legionnaire. He'd have been a sculptor. And because it was so low down it wasn't a repair, but part of the original building programme. My mind kept going back to my Incas, or the possibility of one of these guys turning up in northern Britain in about AD120. Somebody would have had to abduct him from the Andes of Peru cAD1450, and transport him back in time by 1,330 years, and drop him down in Britain. Impossible, I hear you say—and I agree with you entirely—though there's still that but!

For good measure, there is one other but. Most of us have heard of the Nasca lines in Peru. These are straight lines running from horizon to horizon. They take the shape of animals and insects, but can only be seen and fully understood from the air. The big question has always been, why draw something out that can't be seen by the people on the ground who make them? A complete mystery—yet to make matters worse we in Britain have exactly the same problem, which no one has mentioned before. The White Horse of Uffington, on the Ridgeway, can only be fully viewed aerially, which is evident from every photo or postcard. If you walk along the Ridgeway, it's difficult to see other than a few bare patches. You can walk down the hill to the road below, and you'll see more of it, even to the extent of discerning the shape of the hind quarters of a Celtic horse—but you can't see the whole unless you have wings. So, there you are—and as Herodotus would say, I don't believe in visiting aliens, but you can if you will!